A Jaina Perspective on the Philosophy of Religion

kevalajñana or perfect knowledge and "to the perfect consciousness the whole reality is obvious". Yet, significantly, such a being or Arhat is not God, no matter how analogous to one he (or she) might be made to appear.[1] Similarly, to the extent that philosophy of religion is characterised not by revelatory but rational investigation into the nature of reality, it too, like Jaina philosophy, should not be confused with revealed theology.

Christian theology, however, also developed the notion of natural theology, along with that of revealed theology. The program of natural theology "was to demonstrate rationally the existence of God, thus preparing the way for the claims of revelation".[2] It should be obvious by now that neither Jaina philosophy nor the philosophy of religion supports such a programme. Jaina philosophy may be said to be naturalistic in the sense that it philosophically investigates, with considerable thoroughness, the nature of the natural world.[3] Such an investigation, however, does not in any way imply a natural theology.

Apologetics refers to the "philosophical defense of religious beliefs". There is a branch of Jaina studies, to be sure, which is best described as Jaina apologetics.[4] It must, however, be distinguished from Jaina philosophy, just as apologetics itself must be carefully distinguished from the philosophy of religion.

Philosophy of religion, then, as well as Jaina philosophy, must be distinguished from rational theology, revealed theology, natural theology and apologetics and they must be understood on their own terms as "*philosophical thinking about religion*",[5] in the latter case from the perspective of Jainism. One might, however, ask: what does such thinking more precisely entail? John Hick explains what it does and does not entail as follows:

> What is the philosophy of religion? It was at one time generally understood to mean religious philosophizing in the

1. *Ibid.*, p. 331.
2. John H. Hick, *Philosophy of Religion* (fourth edition)(Englewood Cliffs, New Jersey: Prentice Hall, 1990) p. 1.
3. K.P. Sinha, *The Philosophy of Jainism* (Calcutta: Punthi Pustak, 1990) Chapter Two.
4. Wm. Theodore de Bary, ed., *Sources of Indian Tradition* (New York: Columbia University Press, 1958) Vol. I, p. 83.
5. John H. Hick, *op. cit.*, p. 1.

> sense of the philosophical defense of religious convictions. It was seen as continuing the work of "natural," distinguished from "revealed," theology. Its program was to demonstrate rationally the existence of God, thus preparing the way for the claims of revelation. But it seems better to call this endeavor "natural theology" and to term the wider philosophical defense of religious beliefs "apologetics." Then we may reserve the name "philosophy of religion" for what (by analogy with philosophy of science, philosophy of art, etc.) is its proper meaning, namely, *philosophical thinking about religion.*[1]

What is Religion?

We know that the philosophical method consists of rational investigation. But how do we define the subject to which it is meant to be applied, namely, religion?

The question of defining, or even describing, religion has bedevilled the field of religious studies for a long time and scholars have virtually despaired of devising a definition which might be universally acceptable.[2] John Hick suggests a way of reconciling various types of definitions of religion, such as the phenomenological, the psychological, the sociological, the naturalistic, etc., by proposing the "perhaps... more realistic view...that the word 'religion' does not have a single correct meaning, but that the many different phenomena subsumed under it are related in the way that...philosopher Ludwig Wittgenstein...characterised as family resemblance".[3] Wittgenstein illustrates his point with the help of the word "game". A game cannot be defined as 'being played for pleasure (for some are played for profit), or as being competitive (for some are solo performances), or as requiring skill (for some depend on chance), or indeed it would seem by any single feature'. Yet the fact that these games cannot be defined in terms of a unifying characteristic does not necessarily mean that they do not hang together. For "all these different kinds of game overlap in character with some other kinds, which in turn overlap in different

1. *Ibid.*, emphasis supplied.
2. *Ibid.*, p. 2. Also see Winston L. King "Religion" in Mircea Eliade, Editor in Chief, *The Encyclopedia of Religion* (New York: The Macmillan Company, 1987) Vol. 12, pp. 282-293; etc.
3. John H. Hick, *op. cit.*, p. 2.

ways with yet other kinds, so that the whole ramifying collection hangs together in a complex network of similarities and differences which Wittgenstein likened to the resemblances and differences appearing within a family".[1]

This concept of family resemblance can be applied to the concept of religion with profit, for it allows for differences among religions as well as among definitions of religions to be recognized, without having to give up using the term altogether.

This family-resemblance approach to the definition of religion, it has been argued, is in fact *particularly* applicable to the religions of Indian origin:[2] Hinduism, Buddhism, Jainism and Sikhism–which share some common features and yet differ from one another in significant ways. There is, in fact, some empirical evidence to suggest that Jainas themselves implicitly adopt this approach in certain contexts. It has been pointed out, for instance, that

> The relationship between the Jaina and Hindu traditions has been somewhat ambiguous in post-independence India. While the religious identity of the Jainas has not been compromised, their legal and social identities are somewhat blurred. Since India does not have a uniform civil code, Jainas and Sikhs are included under the Hindu family law. Thus, marriage, divorce, and inheritance are all governed by the law applying to Hindus. Legal texts observe that the courts in India have always applied the Hindu law to Jaina cases in the absence of a Jaina custom that directly contradicts the Hindu law.
>
> Socially, some Jainas in India and especially in the diaspora, while proud of their heritage and identity, simply identify themselves as 'Hindu' when asked about their religion. They do this, they say, because many Westerners are not familiar with the Jaina tradition and the explanations seem tedious in a casual conversation. Interestingly, while these Jainas seem comfortable identifying themselves as Hindu to social

1. *Ibid.*
2. Gavin Flood, "Hinduism, Vaisnavism, and ISCKON: Authentic Traditions or Scholarly Constructions?" *ISCKON Communications Journal* 3:2 (December 1995) p. 7.

acquaintances, they are quite clear about their distinctive religious identity at home and among close friends.[1]

Religion and Soteriology

Although Professor Hick favours the family-resemblance approach to the definition of religion in general, he does proceed to identify one feature which he considers "extremely widespread though not universal" within that "ramifying set of family resemblances"[2] one has chosen to call religion. He identifies it as follows:

> This is a concern with what is variously called salvation or liberation. This is probably not a feature of 'primitive' or 'archaic' religion, which is more concerned with keeping things on an even keel, avoiding catastrophe. However, all the great developed world faiths have a soteriological (from the Greek *soteria,* salvation) structure. They offer a transition from a radically unsatisfactory state to a limitlessly better one. They each speak in their different ways of the wrong or distorted or deluded character of our present human existence in its ordinary, unchanged condition. It is a 'fallen' life, lived in alienation from God; or it is caught in the world-illusion of *maya;* or it its pervaded throughout by *dukkha,* radical unsatisfactoriness. They also proclaim, as the basis for their gospel, that the Ultimate, the Real, the Divine, with which our present existence is out of joint, is good, or gracious, or otherwise to be sought and responded to; the ultimately real is also the ultimately valuable. Completing the soteriological structure, they each offer their own way to the Ultimate–through faith in response to divine grace or through total self-giving to God; or through the spiritual discipline and maturing which leads to enlightenment and liberation. In each case, salvation or liberation consists of a new and limitlessly better quality of existence which comes about in the transition from self-centeredness to Reality-centeredness.[3]

1. Vasudha Narayanan, *op. cit.*, p. 169-170.
2. John Hick, *op. cit.*, p. 3.
3. *Ibid.*, p. 3.

This observation is of considerable interest from the point of view of Jaina philosophy, for Jainism has often been described as a "primitive" or "archaic" religion. Consider, for instance, the following comments:

> The Jainas assume the existence of only one world system, and the *archaism* of their teaching reveals itself in the fact that even liberation is still located within it—at the top of the universe.
>
> ...
>
> But since eternity, the souls are caught up in *samsāra*, the cycle of rebirth. Here again the *archaism* of Jaina thought reveals itself, because the reason of the Jīva's entanglement in samsāra—also here styled *karma*—is actually conceived of as being loaded by heavy matter (*karma*) which pushes it downwards into the heavens, human world or even hells.[1]

Quite a Shamanic view, it would appear. Even S. Radhakrishnan regards Jainism as "the product of an age of immature philosophizing,"[2] while some scholars do not hesitate to characterize some aspects of it as primitive. A.L Basham writes: "For all the subtlety with which many of its doctrines have been elaborated, the *primitive* heritage of Jainism is very evident. It retains characteristics of a stage in the evolution of Indian thought when no entity could be conceived of except on the analogy of solid matter and when everything which moved and every object showing some degree of organization was thought of as being alive. Thus for the Jaina the soul, which is identified with the life (jīva), is *finite and has variable though definite size and weight.* Moreover, *primitive* animistic ideas must have originally inspired the Jaina's attribution of life to entities and objects not thought to be living by other Indian sects".[3]

---

1. Friedhelm Hardy, ed., *The World's Religions: The Religions of Asia* (London: Routledge, 1990) p. 57, emphasis on archaism supplied.
2. S. Radhakrishnan, *op. cit.*, Vol. II, p. 335. He also notes elsewhere: "Colebrooke... contends that Jainism is *older* than Buddhism, since it adopts the animistic belief that nearly everything possessed a soul" (*ibid.*, p. 291, emphasis added).
3. A.L. Basham, "Jainism", in R.C. Zaehner, ed., *The Concise Encyclopedia of Living Faiths* (Boston: Beacon Press, 1954) p. 262, emphasis added.

I have dwelt on this point at some length because if we accept the characterization of Jainism as a "primitive" and "archaic" religion, then it provides a remarkable counter-example to Professor John Hick's general thesis that primitiveness and soteriology do not go together. Jainism possesses an unambiguous soteriological structure.

CHAPTER I

THE CONCEPT OF GOD

God is one of the central concepts in the philosophy of religion, and has a cluster of concepts associated with it. Prominent among these are those of God as one; as infinite and self-existent; as creator; as personal; as loving and good; and as holy.

Monotheism

A number of terms, of which monotheism is one, have been used in relation to God or to describe various forms of belief in God. Prominent among these are: *atheism*: absence of belief in God; *agnosticism*: indeterminacy regarding belief in God; *skepticism*: doubting belief in God.; *naturalism*: accounting for existence in terms of Nature rather than God; *deism*: God as initiating but not regulating creation; *polytheism*: belief in many gods; *henotheism*: allegiance to one God without denying existence of others; *pantheism*: all is God; *panentheism*: God is all and more; and *monotheism*: belief in one God.

It might not be without interest to consider this checklist in the light of Jaina thought.

Atheism: Jainism is atheistic in the sense that it does not believe in one God but it does believe in gods, with a small g. These are "only embodied souls like men and animals, different from them in degree but not in kind."[1]

Agnosticism and Skepticism: Agnosticism in relation to God is not found in Jainism. It resorts to denial rather than prevarication in relation to God. The agnostic attitude, however, need not be confined to God. It can be extended to certain other kinds of metaphysical questions. Thus a religious figure called Sañjaya is identified in Buddhist literature, who basically claimed that if he

1. S. Radhakrishnan, *op. cit.*, Vol. I, p. 331.

knew the answers to certain perplexing questions he would be happy to share them with the interlocutor, but as he does not know the answers, he can't. This Sañjaya is identified by A.L. Basham as a sceptic[1] but by B.K. Matilal as an agnostic[2], who also sees some truth in the claim that Mahāvīra's system of conditional predication "was established in opposition to the 'agnosticism' of Sañjaya".[3]

Naturalism: Jainism explains in terms of Nature what other systems often explain in terms of God. A.L. Basham notes: "Jainism, though not denying the existence of superhuman beings, is fundamentally atheistic. Moreover, it never compromised with theism, or devised a pantheon of substitute gods, as did Mahāyāna Buddhism. From the earliest times to the present day Jainas have strenuously rejected the doctrine that the universe is created or guided by a divine will or divine mind—for them natural law is a sufficient explanation".[4]

Deism and Theism: These play little role in Jaina thought. The universe is viewed as self-regulating and without beginning and end.

Polytheism: Jainism is polytheistic in the sense of accepting the existence of gods, rather than God.

Henotheism, Pantheism, Panentheism: These belong to "none of the above" category on the Jaina theistic checklist.

Monotheism: As stated earlier, the Jainas do not believe in the existence of a God but they do give reasons for not doing so, which will be considered at the appropriate point.

If the question of the existence of God, however, is extended to include God-like beings into consideration, then room is created for further elaboration of the Jaina position.[5] One of the roles of God in Hindu theism is to guarantee the infallibility of revelation. Thus according to "Gotama, the author of *Nyāya-sūtra*, the infallibility of the Veda is due to the infallibility of its speaker or

1. *Ibid.*
2. Bimal Krishna Matilal, *The Central Philosophy of Jainism* (*Anekānta-vāda*) (Ahmedabad: L.D. Institute of Indology, 1981) p. 48.
3. *Ibid.*
4. A.L. Basham, "Jainism and Buddhism", in Wm. Theodore de Bary, ed., *op. cit.*, Vol.I, p. 78.
5. For more support for this perspective see John Cort, "Jain Questions and Answers: Who is God and How Is He Worshipped?" in Daniel S. Lopez, Jr., *Religions of India in Practice* (Princeton, New Jersey: Princeton University Press, 1995) pp. 598-601.

revealer, i.e. Īśvara [God]. Kaṇāda, the author of *Vaiśeṣika-Sūtra* also holds the same view. The Jainas do not admit such an Īśvara, but they hold that the liberated beings becoming *arhats* or *tīrthankaras* are the most perfect beings and, hence, the best teachers. The teachings of the *tīrthankaras* are called the Jaina *Veda* and are regarded as infallible by the Jainas. Jainism is thus not opposed to the doctrine of a Veda-teacher".[1] This point will be developed further in the chapter on revelation. In this chapter one may review the concept of God in relation to Jainism more accommodatingly. Should such an attitude be adopted, one is led to the following comment of S. Radhakrishnan:

> Though there is no such being distinct from the world called God, yet certain of the elements of the world when properly developed obtain deification. These are the arhats, the supreme lords, the omniscient souls who have overcome all faults. Though there is no divine creative spirit, still every soul when it reaches its highest perfection becomes a Paramātman or supreme soul. God is only the highest, noblest and fullest manifestation of the powers which lie latent in the soul of man. All perfect men are divine, and there is no rank among them, since all are equal.[2]

The point can be pursued further, at least in the Indic context. Following K.P. Sinha, one could distinguish between two Jaina attitudes towards Īśvara or God as conceptualized in the Indic world based on whether the concept is accepted in a primary and/or a secondary sense. It could then be maintained that while Jaina philosophy denies Īśvara in a primary sense, a plausible case could be made for the "acceptance of Īśvara in a secondary sense". Sinha also notes, like Radhakrishnan: "It is, therefore, clear that the concept of the liberated self of the Jainas very well resembles that of Īśvara of the theistic schools. Accordingly, the Jainas should not be regarded as atheists in the strict sense of the term, as they accept the existence of some *Īśvara* or *paramātman* in their own sense."[3] He then goes on to say:

1. K.P. Sinha, *op. cit.*, p. 148.
2. S. Radhakrishnan, *op. cit.*, Vol. I, p. 331.
3. K.P. Sinha, *op. cit.*, p. 149.

The difference between the concept of *Īśvara* of the theists and that of *paramātman* of the Jainas is this: the Īśvara of the theists is the creator and governor of the world. He is eternally perfect, his perfect nature being never obscured or limited by his cosmic activities. He is ever-free, since he is never subjected to bondage. Further, he is one and the highest; there is none equal to or higher than Īśvara. The *paramātman* of the Jainas, on the other hand, is unable to create and govern the world. He is not eternally perfect, because during his worldly existence or before the attainment of liberation, he is subjected to bondage. Again, he is not one but many. The Jainas hold that the state of *paramātman* is nothing but the highest, noblest and fullest manifestation of the intrinsic nature of the self. Each self can become *paramātman* by self-culture and self-effort. And, as the selves are many, according to the Jainas, the *paramātmans* are also numerous.[1]

Infinite, Self-existent

The self-subsistence, which, in theism, is ascribed to God, is assigned to Nature in Jaina philosophy, in contrast to God. It is stated that if the "world-process...is mechanical, there is no need for admitting an unseen God lying beyond the world, for we can very well explain this process by attributing this mechanism to the world itself i.e. by holding that the world comes into being and goes on by its own intrinsic nature".[2]

1. *Ibid.*, p. 149. The point may be developed still further as follows: "It is clear from Jaina metaphysics that there is no place in Jainism for God as a creator and distributor of prizes and punishments. By God Jainism understands a liberated soul as well as the *Tīrthankaras*, who provide the highest spiritual ideals to which every soul can aspire: in this sense God is an example to inspire and to guide. Thus the Jaina conception of God is very different from that in Hinduism. Though God is not a creator, the Jaina religion lacks neither devotional fervour nor ceremonial rituals. Jainas offer prayers to him, worship him both in concept and in concrete form as an image, and meditate on him. Respectful prayers are offered to the *Tīrthankara*, the liberated soul, the preceptor, the preacher, and the monk, because these represent various stages of the soul's spiritual progress. Such a routine keeps the Jaina vigilant in pursuit of his ideal and strengthens his heart, constantly reminding him that he must depend on himself to destroy the *karmas*" (A.N. Upadhye, "Jainism", in A.L. Basham, ed., *A Cultural History of India* [Delhi: Oxford University Press, 1975] p. 108-109).
2. K.P. Sinha, *op. cit.*, p. 146.

It could be objected here, however, that the self-existence implied here is within the world, while that of God is outside it. The Jainas themselves distinguish between "eternal time, without form, with beginning or end, and relative time, with beginning and end and variations of hour, minutes, etc. The former is called kāla and the latter samaya".[1] If we apply this distinction to our discussion, then, God's existence will have to be connected with *kāla*. It may be worth noting here that

> The concept of self-existence,' as it occurs in the work of the great theologians, contains two elements:
>
> 1. God is not dependent either for existence or for characteristics upon any other reality. God has not been created by any higher being. There is nothing capable either of constituting or of destroying God. God just is, in infinite richness and plenitude of being as the ultimate, unconditioned, all-conditioning reality. In abstract terms, God has absolute ontological independence.
>
> 2. It follows from this that God is eternal, without beginning or end. If God had a beginning, there would have to be a prior reality to bring God into being; and in order for God's existence to be terminated, there would have to be some reality capable of effecting this. Each of these ideas is excluded by God's absolute ontological independence.[2]

In Jaina philosophy, however, instead of *kāla* being an attribute of God it becomes a category in itself, in keeping with its pluralistic realism.[3] In fact, it is even argued, in relation to the first understanding of aseity that "Īśvara is said to be self-subsistent, but if he were so, why should he produce the world of spirits and matter?"[4]

Creator

In Western thought, God plays a major role as a creator in at least three ways: (1) God creates out of nothing (*creatio ex nihilo*); (2) there

1. S. Radhakrishnan, *op. cit.*, Vol. I, p. 816-817.
2. John H. Hick, *op. cit.*, p. 8.
3. "Time is a necessary category of existence." Appaswami Chakravarti, "Jainism: Its Philosophy and Ethics" in Haridas Bhattacharyya, ed., *The Cultural Heritage of India* (Calcutta: The Ramakrishna Mission Institute of Culture, 1958) Vol. I, p. 425-426.
4. K.P. Sinha, *op. cit.*, p. 147.

is a firm dividing line between the creation and its creator and (3) creation involves time, either in Aquinas's sense that although an eternal universe is theoretically possible, it is scripturally declared to have been created at a point in time or in the Augustinian sense that "creation did not take place *in* time but that time is itself an aspect of the world".

If Western philosophy works from creator to creation; Jaina philosophy works from creation to creator—and never quite gets there. According to Jainism the universe is beginningless, so there is no question of *creatio ex nihilo*; and as there is no creator, there is no question of its sharp disjunction from creation. Creation, though, does involve time. As for the precise role of time, "since the concrete world cannot be dismissed as illusory, the category of time must be postulated as a necessary condition of change" within *it*. The universe is timeless, but the universal process involves time.

Such a view makes it very difficult to connect creation with a creator. The difficulties involved are presented in general terms in the following account:

> Some foolish men declare that Creator made the world.
> The doctrine that the world was created is ill-advised, and should be rejected.
>
> If God created the world, where was he before creation?
> If you say he was transcendent then, and needed no support, where is he now?
>
> No single being had the skill to make this world—
> For how can an immaterial god create that which is material?
>
> How could God have made the world without any raw material?
> If you say he made this first, and then the world, you are faced with an endless regression.
>
> If you declare that this raw material arose naturally you fall into another fallacy,
> For the whole universe might thus have been its own creator, and have arisen equally naturally.

If God created the world by an act of his own will, without any raw material,
Then it is just his will and nothing else — and who will believe this silly stuff?
If he is ever perfect and complete, how could the will to create have arisen in him?
If, on the other hand, he is not perfect, he could no more create the universe than a potter could.

If he is formless, actionless, and all-embracing, how could he have created the world?
Such a soul, devoid of all modality, would have no desire to create anything.

If he is perfect, he does not strive for the three aims of man,
So what advantage would he gain by creating the universe?

If you say that he created to no purpose, because it was his nature to do so, then God is pointless.
If he created in some kind of sport, it was the sport of a foolish child, leading to trouble.

If he created because of the karma of embodied beings [acquired in a previous creation]
He is not the Almighty Lord, but subordinate to something else...

If out of love for living things and need of them he made the world,
Why did he not make creation wholly blissful, free from misfortune?

If he were a transcendent he would not create, for he would be free;
Nor if involved in transmigration, for then he would not be almighty.

Thus the doctrine that the world was created by God
Makes no sense at all.

And God commits great sin in slaying the children whom he himself created.
If you say that he slays only to destroy evil beings, why did he create such beings in the first place?...

Good men should combat the believer in divine creation, maddened by an evil doctrine.

Know that the world is uncreated, as time itself is, without beginning and end,
And is based on the principles of Jainism, life and the rest.

Uncreated and indestructible, it endures under the compulsion of its own nature,
Divided into three sections—hell, earth, and heaven.[1]

See Wm. Theodore de Bary, ed., *op. cit.*, Vol. I, pp. 79-81. For the argument in full philosophical flight see the summary of Guṇaratna's position (Narendra Nath Bhattacharyya, *Jain Philosophy: Historical Outline* [New Delhi: Munshiram Manoharlal Publishers Pvt. Ltd. 1976] pp. 106-108):

Guṇaratna says that for the sake of argument the controversy concerning the perceptibility of God can even be given up, but still it will be impossible for the theist to prove that God causes the world. There is no conceivable explanation of *how actually God can cause it.* If it is said that God causes the world by virtue of his mere being or existence, this logic is clearly untenable, because if existence is the only criterion, there is nothing to prevent the conception of the potter also causing the world. If it is said that God causes the world by virtue of his possession of knowledge, the Yogins also may be viewed as causing the world, because they are supposed to possess great knowledge. If it is said that God causes the world by virtue of his being characterised by knowledge, will and effort, it is quite illogical because without a body he cannot be the substratum of knowledge etc. It is said that God causes the world by virtue of the 'functional intermediacy' (*Vyāpāra*) of knowledge, etc., like the third alternative here also the vexed question regarding God's body will arise. It is said that God causes the world by virtue of his divinity, it is also fallacious because the implication of the term divinity is not at all clear. Then again we are confronted by another question regarding the motive that leads God to create the world. If god creates the world out of purely personal whim, it leads to the possibility of creation being at least occasionally imperceptible, because something done to satisfy a purely personal whim is not necessarily meant for public exhibition. If God creates the world under the guidance of the destiny of the individual souls, he loses his independence. If he creates the world out of compassion, everything of the world then would have been pleasant. If God creates the world for sport, and

Personal

The Western concept of God is highly personal. But in Jainism one is exhorted to the realization: "Man! Thou art thine own friend; why wishest thou for a friend beyond thyself?... It is possible for us to evade the effects of karma by extraordinary exertions. Nor is there any interference by God. The austere heroes are blessed not because of the uncertain whims of a capricious God, but by the order of the universe of which they themselves are part".[1]

It may be helpful to distinguish here between the "personal" and "a person". John Hick points out that

> Most theologians speak of God as "personal" rather than as "a Person". The latter phrase suggests the picture of a magnified human individual. (Thinking of the divine in this way is called anthropomorphism, from the Greek *anthropos*, man, and *morphe*, shape—"in the shape of man".) The statement that God is personal is accordingly intended to signify that God is "at least personal", that whatever God may be

for rewarding and punishing, he is characterised by attachment and hatred. If God creates the world because of inherent nature (*Svabhāva*), the unconscious world then may as well be conceived as coming to being because of inherent nature, and not because of his action.

According to Guṇaratna any probans that may be cited to prove God as the cause of the world must necessarily be contradictory, because the corroborative instance will always indicate an embodied and non-omniscient cause. Any rendering used to infer God as the cause of the world must also suffer from the fallacy of the 'counter-acted' (*prakaraṇa-sama* or *satpratipakṣa*), i.e. the fallacy of allowing scope for a counter-inference to prove the opposite of the desired thesis. God cannot be eternal, because only by virtue of some transformation of his own nature [alone] can God be conceived as the cause of the world. His knowledge also cannot be eternal, for this is contradicted by both perception and inference. God cannot be omniscient because there is no concomitance between the varieties of worldly objects and omniscience.

The Jain attitude towards the conception of God thus finds a nice expression in the polemical but hair-splitting analysis of Guṇaratna. If by God is understood a supreme personality responsible for the creation of the world, Jainism must be declared to be atheistic, since it deliberately rejects such a conception of divinity as self-discrepant. If God needs to create the world, it means that he feels a want which is inconsistent with his necessary perfection as the Supreme. So there is no God, and the world was never created. The Universe has neither any beginning nor any end, and hence any conception of God as creator is absolutely unnecessary.

1. S. Radhakrishnan, *op. cit.*, Vol. I, p. 327.

> beyond our conceiving, God is not less than personal, not a mere it, but always the higher and transcendent divine Thou.[1]

It was pointed out earlier, however, that "the concept of the liberated self of the Jainas very well resembles that of Īśvara of the theistic schools. Accordingly, the Jainas should not be regarded as atheists in the strict sense of the term, as they accept the existence of some *Īśvara* or *paramātman* in their own sense".[2] If we accept this equation then it produces a curious result: that while this 'God' of the Jainas is and cannot be *personal*, it is always a *person*!

Loving, Good

God is portrayed as loving in Christian thought. This love is of a special kind. The English word love doubles for two Greek words: *eros* and *agape*. Eros is the love which has an admixture of desire in it; when thus mixed with sexual desire it has the meaning it has in the word *erotic*. But the love denoted by the word *agape* has the effect of excluding people from becoming an object of each other's sexual desire, without excluding affection. Inasmuch as *agape* values people for who they are in themselves, as against what they might be to us, the love of God towards mankind is characterised by *agape*. For the Jaina, however, such love might well smack of partiality.

In Jainism, the *jinas*, whom we earlier in some ways equated with God, are beyond 'passion' of any kind – whether *eros* or *agape*. And God as such does not exist according to Jainism, but gods (with a small g) do and they are capable of watching over us. In a sense then, although *God* and love are severed; love in a sense continues to be associated with the gods, though neither with *God* on account of the absence of its existence, or with the *jinas*, on account of the mode of their existence. Even here the Jaina attitude affects the implication of this love. For although the gods "hear the prayers and bestow favours" yet "so far as the Jinas are concerned the best mode of worshipping them is to accept their advice".[3]

---

1. John H. Hick, *op. cit.*, p.11.
2. K.P. Sinha, *op. cit.*, p. 149.
3. S. Radhakrishnan, *op. cit.*, Vol. I, p. 332.

In Christianity, goodness runs into a problem in relation to God. As John Hick asks:

> Does that belief imply a moral standard external to God, in relation to which God can be said to be good? Or alternatively, does it mean that God is good by definition, so that God's nature, whatever it may be, is the norm of goodness?
>
> Either position involves difficulties. If God is good in relation to some independent standard of judgment, God is no longer the sole ultimate reality, but exists in a moral universe whose character is not divinely ordained. If, however, God is good by definition, and it is a tautology that whatever God commands is right, other implications arise which are hard to accept.[1]

This dilemma does not have to be faced in Jainism because the *good* has no relation to God. However, in avoiding the theistic dilemma, Jainism can be said to create its own karmic dilemma in relation to goodness. Kosheya Walli notes, for instance, that the great Jaina thinker "Kundakunda... has shown that Jiva or soul and Ajiva or non-soul are the most important categories to be carefully studied. It is observed that though there is a distinction between good and evil karma, *the real fact is that the distinction is meaningless from the supreme point of view inasmuch as karma itself is a source of bondage and has to be avoided*".[2]

The Christian idea of the goodness of God is combined with that of his 'wrath'. John Hick mentions how C.H. Dodd takes much of its thunder away by pointing out that the expression is "used in a curiously impersonal way to refer to the inevitable reaction of the divinely appointed moral order of the universe upon wrong doing".[3] Jaina philosophy would approve of this trend of thought, though it may be inclined to change "divinely" to "naturally" appointed order. However, some descriptions of karmic conse-

---

1. John H. Hick, *op. cit.*, p. 12.
2. Koshelya Walli, *Theory of Karman in Indian Thought* (Varanasi: Bharata Manisha, 1977) p. 255-256, emphasis added. The resolution of the dilemma too may be similar in both cases, that is to say, "frankly circular" (see John H. Hick, op. cit., p.12).
3. *Ibid.*, p. 13.

quences in Jaina literature seem so overblown that one is almost tempted to speak of the *wrath of karma*, as in the following instance: "A tenth-century book, the Yaśatilaka, describes the harm that befalls a prince who sacrifices a rooster made of dough instead of a live bird. Although a live being was not killed, nevertheless the intention of harm was present in the act".[1] At the same time, given the Jaina penchant for non-violence, one can imagine how off-putting Jainas might find a concept or an expression like the 'wrath of God'.

A few words on the grace of God may not be out of place in the present context, to balance, as it were, the reference to his wrath. The problem to which the grace of God answers is that of how a soul—either corrupted as in Christianity or enmeshed in karma as in Hinduism—is capable of a soteriological turning-around, given its unpromising situation in this regard. Now "most Indian traditions...have dealt with these problems by recourse to a theistic doctrine; the intervention of some divine agency is here seen to provide the 'helping hand' that lifts human souls from the mire of transmigration".[2] From the Jaina point of view, however, this solution, or the analogous Christian solution by extension, generates

> even more logical problems than it solved. The agent of grace, it was said, would have to be a special sort of being (*purusa-viśeṣa*), unlike all other living things in that it has been forever free of bondage (*sadā-mukta*). But how could an unbound being ever come into contact with the world of saṁsāra—or influence it—since such actions are by definition limited to the embodied state? If it is admitted, moreover, that even a single being can exist outside the framework of karmic entrapment, that same possibility must be admitted for any number of other beings as well. Thus one would be driven into the theory that all souls are *in reality* unbound, and that we must understand "bondage" as illusory. But if this is so, if bondage is unreal, then why is there the experience of suffering?[1]

1. Vasudha Narayanan, *op. cit.*, p. 153.
2. Padmanabh S. Jaini, *The Jaina Path of Purification*, (Berkeley: University of California Press, 1979) p. 135.
3. *Ibid.*, p. 136.

Holy

God is of course the supreme embodiment of holiness in the Judaic-Christian tradition. This holiness is memorably commemorated in the following lines by Isaiah:

To whom then will you liken God,
or what likeness compare with him?
The idol! a workman casts it,
and a goldsmith overlays it with gold
and casts for it silver chains.
He who is impoverished chooses for an offering
wood that will not rot;
he seeks out a skillful craftsman
to set up an image that will not move.
Have you not known? Have you not heard?
Has it not been told you from the beginning?
Have you not understood from the foundations of the earth?
It is he who sits above the circle of the earth,
and its inhabitants are like grasshoppers;
who stretches out the heavens like a curtain,
and spreads them like a tent to dwell in;
who brings princes to nought,
and makes the rulers of the earth as nothing...
To whom then will you compare me,
that I should be like him? says the Holy One.
Lift up you eyes on high and see:
who created these?[1]

Such sentiment are reserved by the Jainas for the Jinas.[2]

1. Cited in John H. Hick, *op. cit.*, pp. 13-14.
2. Vasudha Narayanan, *op. cit.*, p. 163-164.

CHAPTER II

THE CASE FOR GOD

The case for God is traditionally made through a series of arguments. One may now proceed to first recapitulate and then examine them in the light of Jaina thought.

The Ontological Argument

The ontological argument is encapsulated in the famous statement of Anselm that God is "a being than which nothing greater can be conceived".[1] John Hick hastens to add: "It is clear that by 'greater' Anselm means more perfect, rather than spatially bigger".[2] It is a point of some interest, that by changing the expression 'spatially bigger' to 'spatially *higher*', this ontological argument could perhaps be pressed into service of Jaina philosophy. The situation of the Jina as visualised in its perfect state in Jainism will have to be considered in order to render the suggestion plausible. This involves a description of the process of emancipation of the soul as visualized in Jainism. This process of emancipation in its final stages may be described as follows:

> It is from the human form, therefore, that the soul undertakes its final task: elimination of those activities (yoga) which necessarily accrue to the condition of embodiment. Here at last are employed the third and fourth types of śukladhyāna, to which the kevalin resorts just a few moments before physical death. In the trance called *sūkṣmakriyā-anivartin* (the state of subtle movement), all gross and subtle activities of mind and speech, as well as the gross activities of the body, are absolutely stopped. There now remain only the autonomic processes: breathing, heartbeat, and the like. Even

1. John H. Hick, *op. cit.*, p. 15.
2. *Ibid.*

> these are brought to cessation by attainment of the highest meditational state, *vyuparatakriyā-anivartin,* (absolute nonmotion). Both of these dhyānas are designated as *anivartin,* meaning 'that from which there can be no falling back'.[1]

Finally, "the soul *must* proceed from the state of subtle movement into that of nonmovement, the latter being identical with the fourteenth guṇasthāna (ayoga-kevali–isolated from all ghātiyā karmas and free of all activities). This guṇasthāna lasts only for an instant; suddenly, as the āyu karmas are exhausted and death occurs, the soul leaves the body, *darting upward by its very nature to the highest point of the universe* (*loka-ākāśa*). There it will reside, totally free of either bondage or movement, for all eternity".[2]

The Jina, on account of having completely shed the karma which weighed the soul down, rises to the top, the summit, of the universe. None can go any higher. This is how the ontological argument applies to him: *He is a being than which nothing higher can be conceived.*

In connection with Anselm's original formulation, John Hick notes an interesting point:

> It is important to notice that the idea of the most perfect conceivable being is different from the idea of the most perfect being that there is. The ontological argument could not be founded upon this latter notion, for although it is true by definition that the most perfect being that there is exists, there is no guarantee that this being is what Anselm means by God. Consequently, instead of describing God as the most perfect being that there is, Anselm describes God as the being who is so perfect that no more perfect can even be conceived.[3]

This also holds for Jainism. It is not claimed in Jainism that the greatest being is one who is on the highest; rather Jainism explicitly states that the Jina is such a being, who adorns the pinnacle by its presence.

1. Padmanabh S. Jaini, *The Jaina Path of Purification,* p. 269-270.
2. *Ibid.*, p. 270, emphasis added.
3. John H. Hick, *op. cit.*, p. 15-16.

Anselm's ontological argument has been philosophically developed in two directions. It is again a matter of some interest that both these forms could be applied to the case of the Jina.

First Form of the Argument

The first form of the argument may be developed by making the distinction between (1) something which only possesses a notional existence, and (2) something which possesses an actual existence. It is clear that, of two things in all other ways alike, the actual one would be considered superior to the notional one. In the somewhat convoluted prose of Anselm this argument is presented as follows:

> If then that-than-which-a-greater-cannot-be-thought exists in the mind alone, this same that-than-which-a-greater-*cannot*-be-thought is that-than which-a-greater-*can*-be-thought. But this is obviously impossible. Therefore there is absolutely no doubt that something-than-which-a-greater-cannot-be-thought exists both in the mind and in reality.[1]

Second Form of the Argument

The second argument defines God in such a way "that it is impossible to conceive of God's not existing", on account of the fact of God's self-existence (*aseity*). In Anselm's words the argument would read as follows:

> For something can be thought to exist that cannot be thought not to exist. Hence, if that-than-which-a-greater-cannot-be-thought can be thought not to exist, then that-than-which-a-greater-cannot-be-thought is not the same as that-than-which-a-greater-cannot-be-thought, which is absurd. Something-than-which-a-greater-cannot-be-thought exists so truly then, that it cannot be even thought not to exist.[2]

It should be apparent that both these forms of the argument can be applied to the Jina. In the first case, if the Jina represents perfection in Jainism, which it does, being referred to as *siddha*

1. Cited, *ibid.*, p. 16.
2. Cited, *ibid.*

or perfect, then surely actualized perfection has to be placed a cut above notional perfection. Similarly, in the case of the second argument, in Jaina thought, although Time plays an important role, such aseity belongs to it[1] rather than to God or even the Jinas.[2] Liberation is eternal in Jainism,[3] but not in the sense of asiety.

Criticisms of the Argument

The criticism and countercriticisms of this argument have a long history and are of considerable interest for the trajectory the argument has assumed.

Gaunilon, a contemporary of Anselm, criticised the argument on the ground that it conflated the realm of reality with that of the imagination. To use an updated version of his example, just because one can conceive of the most perfect conceivable island does not mean that it exists. Just because one can think of a *siddha* does not mean that there is one.

Anselm, in effect, answered this criticism of the argument in the first form, by using its second form and arguing that while a contingent object like an island may not exist, an entity like God would possess necessary existence. In other words: "The most perfect island, so long as it was genuinely an island — 'a piece of land surrounded by water' and thus part of the physical globe — is by definition a dependent reality, which can without contradiction be thought not to exist; and therefore Anselm's principle does not apply to it. It applies only to the most perfect conceivable being, which is defined as having eternal and independent (i.e. necessary) existence. Thus far, then, it would seem that the second from of the argument is able to withstand the criticism."[4]

In Jaina thought, however, although the two arguments can be considered separately, one cannot be used to trump the other, because Jainism is a system of realistic pluralism, in which the world

1. K.K. Dixit, *Jaina Ontolology* (Ahmedabad: L.D. Institute of Indology, 1971) p. 34-35.
2. S.C. Jain, *Structure and Functions of Soul in Jainism* (New Delhi: Bharatiya Jnanapith, 1978) p. 206.
3. Devendra Muni Shastri, *A Source-Book in Jaina Philosophy* (Udaipur: Sri Tarak Guru Jain Granthalaya, 1983) p. 230.
4. John H. Hick, *op. cit.*, p. 17.

—the material world—possesses the same degree of reality as the spiritual. We may wish to question this[1] fundamental ontological (pluralistic) dualism of Jainism but to the extent that we are operating from within the framework of that system, it has to be acknowledged.

John Hick raises the interesting question: "Can Anselm's argument in its first form, however, be defended against Gaunilon's criticism? This depends upon whether the idea of the most perfect conceivable island is a coherent and consistent idea. Is it possible, even in theory, to specify the characteristics of the most perfect conceivable island? This is the question for the reader to consider."[2]

When a Jaina reader considers the question she is likely to be struck by two points. The first is "whether it is possible, in principle, to specify the characteristics of the most perfect conceivable island?" The Jaina response is likely to be that philosophers have not been very successful at carrying out this exercise in relation to God.[3] The second point would pertain to 'whether the idea of the most perfect conceivable island is a coherent and consistent idea'. From a Jaina perspective this puts an ontic premium on coherence and consistency, which may not be justified. Thought is supposed to correspond to fact and not vice versa. For instance, "To the question how an identical object can exhibit different features—how unity and diversity can co-exist, the Jainas reply that our sole warrant for speaking about reality is experience and that when experience vouches for such a character of reality, it must be admitted to be so."[4]

Anselm's argument was later formulated by Descartes in terms of 'existence as a property or predicate'. To illustrate: "just as the fact that its internal angles are equal to two right angles is a necessary characteristic of a triangle, so existence is a necessary characteristic of a supremely perfect being. A triangle without its

1. M. Hiriyanna, *Outlines of Indian Philosophy* (London: Allen & Unwin, 1932), p. 172.
2. *Ibid.*, p. 17.
3. See K.P. Sinha, *op. cit.*, p. 146ff.
4. M. Hiriyanna, *The Essentials of Indian Philosophy* (London: Allen & Unwin, 1949) p. 65.

defining properties would not be a triangle, and God without existence would not be God. The all-important difference is that in the case of the triangle we cannot infer that any triangles exist, since existence is not of the essence of triangularity. However, in the case of a supremely perfect being we can infer existence, for existence is an essential attribute without which no being would be unlimitedly perfect."[1]

This formulation of the argument was criticized by Kant. His criticism may be presented at two levels. At one level, using the illustration of the triangle he said pertinently: "To posit a triangle, and yet to reject its three angles is self-contradictory; but there is no self-contradiction in rejecting the triangle altogether with its three angles. The same holds true of the concept of an absolutely necessary being."[2]

A parallel Jaina argument would run somewhat like this. If the Hindu Vedas assert the existence of God, then it would be contradictory to accept the Vedas and reject God. But there is no logical contradiction involved in rejecting *both.*

At another level, Kant also challenged the idea of God's existence being attached to the concept of God, like three sides to a triangle. He pointed out that "the idea of existence does not add anything to the concept of a particular thing or kind of thing. An imaginary hundred dollars, for example, consists of the same number of dollars as a real hundred dollars. When we affirm that the dollars are real, or exist, we are saying that the concept is instantiated in the world. Thus to say of *x* that it exists in not to say that in addition to its various other attributes it has the attribute of existing, but is to say that there is an *x* in the real world."[3]

The Jaina position sheds interesting light on the issue. It is a

---

1. John H. Hick, op. cit., p. 18.
2. Cited, ibid., p. 18.
3. *Ibid.* He goes on to say (*ibid.*, pp. 18-19): "Essentially the same point has more recently been made by Bertrand Russell in his analysis of the word 'exists.' He has shown that although 'exists' is grammatically a predicate, logically it performs a different function, which can be brought out be the following translation: 'Cows exist' means 'There are *x*'s such that '*x* is a cow' is true.' This translation makes it clear that to say that cows exist is not to attribute a certain quality (namely existence) to cows, but is to assert that there are objects in the world to which the description summarized in the word 'cow'

fundamental Jaina position, which will unfold more fully as the book progresses, that reality is 'manifold', or complex, a doctrine referred to by the term *anekāntavāda.*[1]

> The principle of *anekānta* can be briefly described as the acceptance of the manifoldness of reality. Jaina philosophers claim that no philosophic or metaphysical proposition can be true if it is simply asserted without any condition or limitation. If a proposition is asserted as "x is f" then it becomes *ekānta* 'one-sided.' This means that the proposition ascribes *unconditionally* a predicate-property to the subject and thereby excludes other rival possibilities (contradictory predicates). For Jainism such an unconditional assertion violates the principle of *anekānta.* As far as the Jainas are concerned, if a metaphysical proposition violates this principle, it is to be regarded as false. [2]

And to the extent that God's existence is asserted *unconditionally*, it is falsifiable by making an opposite assertion.[3]

The argument runs into difficulty not only with the Jaina idea of reality but also the Jaina concept of existence. "The Jaina conception of 'existence' (*sat*) was intimately related to their notion of 'substance'. In fact the Jainas redefined the notion of substance, in accordance with their *anekānta* principle, as a combination of the notion of 'being' and 'becoming'".[4] According to Jainism, existence includes both, and God is in danger of falling between these two stools, while the "Jainas explicated their notion

---

applies. Similarly 'Unicorns do not exist' is the equivalent of 'There are no *x*'s such that '*x* is a unicorn' is true.' This way of construing negative existential statements—statements that deny that some particular kind of thing exists—avoids the ancient puzzle about the status of the 'something' of which we assert that it does not exist. Since we can talk about unicorns, for example, it is easy to think that unicorns must in some sense be or subsist or, perhaps, that they inhabit a paradoxical realm of nonbeing or potential being. Russell's analysis, however, makes it clear that 'unicorns do not exist' is not a statement about unicorns but about the concept or description 'unicorn' and is the assertion that this concept has no instances."

1. See A.N. Upadhye, *op. cit.*, pp. 104-105.
2. B.K. Matilal, *op. cit.*, p. 2.
3. *Ibid.*
4. *Ibid.*

of substance in such a way as to avoid falling between the two stools of being and becoming. It was a grand compromise of flux and permanence"[1], with God nowhere in the picture.

The First Cause and Cosmological Arguments

Under this heading let us examine the five ways of establishing the existence of God developed by Aquinas. To recapitulate them briefly: "The first way argues from the fact of change to a Prime Mover; the second from causation to a First Cause; the third from contingent being to a necessary Being; the fourth from degrees of value to Supreme Value; and the fifth from evidences of purposiveness to a Divine Designer."[2]

As for the first way, the Jainas argue that if God is immaterial and without a body, how would He set matter in motion? And if He could do this with supernatural power, then we run into a typically Jaina objection; they will ask: "What [is] this supernatural power... If that power be omniscience, then it cannot be said to have anything to do with creation, because omniscience is not necessarily concomitant with creativity. An *arhat*, for example, is also omniscient, but he cannot create the universe."[3]

As for the second way, "if an intelligent agent of the world is inferred on the strength of the cause-and-effect relation found in the empirical world, then that agent will have to be regarded as an empirical reality. And as no being of the empirical world is perfect and omniscient [God] will have to be regarded as imperfect and unomniscient".[4] At the time of creation, moreover, God will have to be in a state other than and different from in which he did not create. In that case, [God] will have to be regarded [as subject to] an effect, which will require its own cause, *ad infinitum.*

As for the third way, can we speak of contingent being of "atoms of the elements of the earth, etc."which "are regarded as eternal"[5]? Moreover, in Jainism, matter has "certain inalienable features; but

1. *Ibid.*, p. 37.
2. John H. Hick, *op. cit.*, p. 20.
3. K.P. Sinha, *op. cit.*, p. 144.
4. *Ibid.* p. 141.
5. Surendranath Dasgupta, *op. cit.*, Vol. I, p. 203.

within the limits imposed by them it can become anything through qualitative differentiation. The transmutation of elements is quite possible in this view and is not a dream of the alchemist".[1]

As for the fourth way, God is hardly of any value in Jainism, "as is clear from its repudiation of God in the accepted sense. The truth is that the primary aim of Jainism is the perfection of the soul, rather than the interpretation of the universe—a fact which may be supported by the old statement that āśrava and saṁvara [karmic inflow and its termination] constitute the whole of Jaina teaching, the rest being only an amplification of them."[2]

The fifth way will be discussed in the next section.

The Design (or Teleological) Argument

This argument has a distinguished ancestry, running from Plato, through Thomas Aquinas down to William Paley, to whom we owe its popular formulation with the analogy of a watch. Simple objects of nature, like a rock, do not call for an explanation on account of their simplicity, unlike some other objects. Thus "if I see a watch lying on the ground, I cannot reasonably account for it in a similar way. A watch consists of a complex arrangement of wheels, cogs, axles,. springs, and balances, all operating accurately together to provide a regular measurement of the lapse of time. It would be utterly implausible to attribute the formation and assembling of these metal parts into a functioning machine to the chance operation of such factors as wind and rain. We are obliged to postulate an intelligent, mind which is responsible for the phenomenon."[3]

Note that neither the fact that I have never seen a watch before, nor the fact that it may not be in working order, invalidates the argument. What holds for the watch can then be extended to the universe as a complex phenomena—the design pointing to a designer—presumably God.

The Jainas remain unconvinced. They raise the following objections to the argument. (1) If it be held "that the particular arrangement of the different parts of the world forces one to

1. M. Hiriyanna, *Outlines of Indian Philosophy*, p. 162.
2. *Ibid.*, p. 173.
3. John H. Hick, *op. cit.*, p. 23.

assume an intelligent cause", then the Jainas "contradict this by saying that the arrangement and adjustment found in things like jar, cloth, etc. point of course, to some intelligent maker or makers but the order found in the world *as a whole* does not necessarily bring with it the idea of an intelligent creator".[1] To the further argument, that though the two effects are not identical but sufficiently similar, the Jaina would reply that "from similarity no valid inference can follow. Smoke and water-vapour are similar to each other, but inference of fire from water-vapour can never be valid".[2] (2) Even if we grant for the sake of argument that the whole world is an effect, "the Jainas inquire whether here the term effect means 'a general effect' or a 'special effect'".[3]

If the world is regarded as a 'general effect', then it will "not necessarily lead to the supposition of an intelligent cause. An effect points to the existence of a cause, it is true, but it does not necessarily follow from the same concomitance that the cause would be an intelligent being. Our experience does not testify to the fact that every effect must have an intelligent case behind it".

The distinction between general and special effect is of interest here. A wrist watch would be a special effect; wild grain or plants would constitute general effect. As a general effect the world could be, and according to Jainas is, just a brute fact. In the case of a special effect there is the problem of applying the result obtained from a part to the whole. And even if 'general effects' are attributed to an intelligent agency, "it would be impossible to discover any contrary instance".[4] (3) The Jainas also answer the designer argument by what reads like a Darwinian argument: "...if the world-process is said to be mechanical, there is no need of admitting an unseen God lying beyond the world. For we can very well explain this process by attributing this mechanism to the world itself i.e. holding that the world comes into being and goes on by its own intrinsic nature."[5]

1. K.P. Sinha, *op. cit.*, p. 141, emphasis added.
2. Ibid.
3. Ibid., p. 140.
4. Ibid., p. 142.
5. Ibid., p. 146.

Jainism, Theism and Probability

John Hick notes that "Since Hume's time a broader form of design argument has been offered, two generations ago by F.R. Tennant and today by Richard Swinburne. Both claim that when we take account of a sufficiently comprehensive range of data—not only the teleological character of biological evolution but also man's religious, moral, aesthetic, and cognitive experience—it becomes *cumulatively* more probable that there is a God than that there is not. Theism is presented as the most probable world-view or metaphysical system."[1]

For a Jaina response to this view, one might focus on the *cumulative* nature of the evidence pointing to the reality of theism. Jaina epistemology favours a leap rather than a ladder approach to the question of knowing ultimate reality. The knowledge of the *jīva* is no doubt fragmentary;[2] however, a "mere pooling of the contributions of the different standpoints will not lead us to the truth in itself."[3] Thus when John Hick notes, that, while on the one hand, some "thinkers claim that a theistic interpretation of the world is superior to its alternatives because it alone takes adequate account of man's moral and religious experience, as well as giving due place to the material aspects of the universe,"[4] and on the other, that, "this claim is disputed by nontheistic thinkers, who point in particular to the existence of evil as something that fits better into a naturalistic than into a religious philosophy,"[5] then Jainism comes out siding with the latter view.

Given that the case for and against the existence of God is hardly an open-and-shut case, and in fact a closely and hotly contested one, some scholars have tried to induct probability theory into the discussion. Two main theories in this field have been identified: the "frequency" theory and the "reasonableness of belief theory".[6]

Most scholars associate the word probability theory with its "frequency" version, given the vogue of statistics. A standard example

1. John H. Hick, *op. cit.*, p. 26, emphasis added.
2. M. Hiriyanna, *op. cit.*, p. 158.
3. S. Radhakrishnan, *op. cit.*, Vol. I, p. 159.
4. John H. Hick, *op. cit.*, p. 26.
5. *Ibid.*
6. *Ibid.*, p. 26.

of it would be that 'since a die has six faces, each of which is equally likely to fall uppermost, the probability of throwing any one particular number at a given throw is one in six'. The problem with applying this theory to our universe of discourse is the nature of the universe. It is just one (and not six, for example). "If—impossibly—we knew that there were a number of universes (for example, ten) and if in addition we knew that, say, half of them were God-produced and half not, then we could deduce that the probability of our own universe's being God-produced would be one in two. However, since by 'the universe' we mean the totality of all that is (other than any creator of the universe), clearly no reasoning based upon the frequency theory of probability is possible concerning its character."[1]

It is worth noting that this argument may *not* work with the two other religions of Indian origin–Hinduism and Buddhism–because they accept a doctrine of multiple universes. Jainism, by contrast, accepts only one universe and so objection is valid in its case.

We turn next to the "reasonableness of belief theory". According to this theory "to say that statement P is more probable than statement Q is to say that when they are both considered in relation to a common body of prior (evidence-stating) propositions, it is more 'reasonable' to believe P than Q".[2] Even if one disregards the problems associated with what is reasonable, which are bound to be greater in a system like Jainism which believes in the manifold nature of reality than in one which does not, the problem of a single universe queers the pitch here too. "In the unique case of the universe as a whole there is no body of prior evidence-stating propositions to which we can appeal, since all our propositions must be about either the whole or a part of the universe itself. In other words, there is nothing outside the universe that might count as evidence concerning its nature. There is only one universe, and this one and only universe is capable of being interpreted both theistically and nontheistically."[3]

Another tack might be to combine the ideas of probability and reasonableness and to argue "in a sense that operates in everyday

1. *Ibid.*
2. *Ibid.*
3. *Ibid.*

common-sense judgements", "although it is not capable of being mathematically formulated, it is more likely or probable that there is than that there is not a God".[1] The Jaina idea of the manifoldness of reality complicates the issue (apart from the fact that the statement begs the question) for it allows for *many more* possibilities than just these two. Thus the "Jainas are fond of quoting the story of the six blind men, who each laid hand on a different part of the elephant and tried to describe the whole animal. The man who caught the ear thought that the creature resembled a winnowing fan, the holder of the leg imagined that he was clinging to a big round pillar, etc."[2]

The Moral Argument

It is the fundamental claim of the moral argument in its various forms, two of which will be discussed here, that "ethical experience, and particularly one's sense of an inalienable obligation to one's fellow human beings, presupposes the reality of God as in some way the source and ground of this obligation."[3]

First Form

One classic statement of this argument is found in Cardinal Newman, who writes:

> If, as is the case, we feel responsibility, are ashamed, are frightened, at transgressing the voice of conscience, this implies that there is One to whom we are responsible, before whom we are ashamed, whose claims upon us we fear...If the cause of these emotions does not belong to this visible world, the Object of which [the conscientious person's] perception is directed must be Supernatural and Divine.[4]

As John Hick notes, however, this merely begs the question. Exalted vehemence cannot substitute for reasoned evidence and Jainism would concur.

---

1. *Ibid.*
2. S. Radhakrishnan, *op. cit.*, Vol. I, p. 301.
3. John H. Hick, *op. cit.*, p. 28.
4. Cited, *ibid.*

Second form

John Hick introduces this form of the argument with the remark that it is not open to the above "objection, for it is not strictly a proof at all. It consists of the claim that anyone seriously committed to respect moral values as exercising a sovereign claim upon his or her life must thereby implicitly believe in the reality of a transhuman source and basis for these values, which religion calls God. Thus, Immanuel Kant argues that both immortality and the existence of God are 'postulates' of the moral life, i.e., beliefs which can legitimately be affirmed as presuppositions by one who recognizes duty as rightfully laying upon one an unconditional claim."[1]

John Hick's response to this second form of the argument is interesting and runs as follows:

> It seems to the present writer that so long as this contention is not overstated it has a certain limited validity. To recognize moral claims as taking precedence over all other interests, is implicitly, to believe in a reality of some kind, other than the natural world, that is superior to oneself and entitled to one's obedience. This is at least a move in the direction of belief in God, who is known in the Judaic-Christian tradition as the supreme moral reality. But it cannot be presented as a proof of God's existence...

For John Hick then it is a pointer but not a proof.

These views were presented in some detail because the Jaina position on this point is the opposite—that, if anything, other forms of belief than the Jaina, *including the theistic*, undermine belief in ethical responsibility. S. Radhakrishnan has summarized this position well:

> *In metaphysics Jainism is opposed to all theories which do not emphasise ethical responsibility. The ethical interest in human freedom is the determining consideration. The theories of the creation of the world by God*, or its development out of prakṛti or its unreality, are criticised on the ground that they cannot account

1. *Ibid.*, p. 28-29.

> for either the origin or the cessation of suffering. To regard the intelligent subject as the product of the five elements is as fruitless from the ethical point of view as to make out that the variety of the world is a manifold presentation of the one intelligent principle. Moral distinctions lose their value on the hypothesis of the passivity of the soul. To say that the soul is safe in its eternity and the events of the world are the results of the mechanical combination and separation of the elements of existence would take away the initiative from the soul and make moral responsibility meaningless. The fatalist theory that all things are fixed by nature obviously leaves no room for individual effort. Ethical values require that the individual can make or unmake himself in the world, and that the soul has a self-identity which it preserves even in the ultimate condition.[1]

It is the moral persuasiveness of theism, if any, which must determine our belief in God and not vice versa.

---

1. S. Radhakrishnan, *op, cit.*, Vol. I, p. 312, emphasis added.

CHAPTER III

THE CASE AGAINST GOD

Arguments against the existence of God have assumed many forms in modern religious discourse. Two points attract attention almost immediately: that arguments against the existence of God have often taken the form of arguments against *religion* (which is putatively built around the existence of God or other forms of ultimate reality) and that these arguments tend to be reductive, that is to say, they argue that God stands not for the metaphysical being it is supposed to be, but for some other social or psychological or historical reality.

The Historical Theory of Religion

The historical theory of religion, for instance, claims that God, and the religion built around Him, merely reflects a historical circumstance or person or belief, which has been deified. It has thus been claimed that the Middle East, from very ancient times, had myths about the dead God who rose from the dead, like Osiris of Egypt and Tammuz of Mesopotamia. The death and resurrection of Jesus conforms to this historical type and explains Christianity more plausibly than God incarnating Himself to die for the sins of others. We noticed earlier, how, in the case of Jainism, repeated references are made to the antiquity of its beliefs. The word *hylozoism* is often invoked in this context, with the implication that Jaina philosophy does not offer an authentic vision of the universe in the eyes of a Jina, but is to be explained in terms of "a characteristic dogma of the Jains which pervades the whole philosophical system and code of morals... the hylozoistic theory that not only animals and plants, but also the smallest particles of the elements, earth, fire, water and wind, are endowed with souls".[1]

1. Prof. Jacobi, as cited by M. Hiriyanna, *Outlines of Indian Philosophy*, p. 160.

It may or may not be so and such investigations into the 'true' origins of religion must indeed be carried out, even encouraged. However, for the purposes of the kind of enterprise we are engaged in, a religious system will have to be accepted not necessarily as "true" but as true in the eyes of its followers, and to be treated as such. If the philosophical doctrines are presented in such a mutated, if not necessarily a mutilated, way as are not recognizable by the followers of a religion as their own philosophy, then an authentic cross-cultural study of philosophy becomes well-nigh impossible. This is a point of view to which Jainism *is particularly sensitive*, according to which the misrepresentation of someone's point of view is tantamount to violence.[1]

Although it does not explicitly say so, Jainism, in asking us to take every point of view seriously, is perhaps warning us in its own subtle way against falling victim to what is widely known as the genetic fallacy, namely, that by explaining the origin of a philosophical view historically, we have also pronounced on its philosophical soundness.

The Sociological Theory of Religion

According to this, now fairly pervasive, perspective in the study of religion, "God as the source of sacred demand claiming total allegiance of the worshipper, is [to be] accounted for as a reflection of society's absolute claim upon the loyalty of its members".[2] Put more broadly, man has not been created by God, "the human animal... has created God in order to preserve its own social existence".[3]

Both the aspects in which the sociological theory of religion has been presented run into difficulties in the context of Jainism. In the context of the first perspective, that the role of religion is *integrative*, one should note that the Jaina movement *separates* itself from the vast general body of Hinduism.[4] As for the second version which correlates society and God, in Jainism the movement is not

1. B.K. Matilal, *op. cit.*, p. 4, 6.
2. John H. Hick, *op. cit.*, p. 31.
3. *Ibid.*
4. Padmanabh S. Jaini, *The Jaina Path of Purification*, passim.

from outside in but from inside out, so far as Jainism is concerned.. "Sin is not an offence against God, but only against man".[1]

Let us now impart to this perspective a Marxist twist and look upon society not as a whole but composed of classes, with their own special interests. This perspective has actually been used by Jainas, both in ancient and modern times, to criticize the activities of the Hindu priesthood. The Hindu ritual of *śrāddha,* for instance, in which offering made to the departed which are actually consumed by the officiating Brahmins present, has been castigated with mordant wit by Malliea as follows:

> Even through the performance of *śrāddha,* increase in posterity is in the case of most people not found; and...in the case of some, as in that of donkeys, pigs, goats etc., even without performance thereof we see it still more... And...
>
> > "If even to dead beings the *śrāddha* is the cause of satisfaction,
> > Then oil might increase the flame of an extinguished lamp."
>
> If it is said that What is enjoyed by the Brahman accrues to them (i.e., the ancestors), whoever is to agree to that? Since only in the Brahman do we see the fattened bellies; and transference of these into theirs (the ancestors') cannot be espied; and because only on the part of the Brahmans is satisfaction witnessed.[2]

In our own times, Padmanabh S. Jaini remarks:

We have noted the [Hindu] belief that this offering is essential if the parent is to obtain a body suitable for entrance into the *pitr-loka,* and hence to gain the chance for eventual rebirth. It is further believed that failure of a son to perform this ritual will result in the loss of inheritance and in his wife's being rendered barren by the curse of the spirits thus stranded in the disembodied state. The

1. S. Radhakrishnan, *op. cit.*, Vol. I, p. 326.
2. Padmanabh S. Jaini, "Karma and the Problem of Rebirth", in Wendy Doniger O'Flaherty, ed., *Karma and Rebirth in Classical Indian Traditions* (Berkeley: University of California Press, 1980) p. 234-235.

śrāddha ritual not only represents a significant expression of the underlying parent-child tensions characteristic of the Indian family but also provides perhaps the most important function of the Brāhmanical castes. The latter point is made in reference to the Brahmins, monopolization of the role of intermediary between the donor and the departed; only if Brahmins consume the offerings can these be "converted" into the material from which the new body of the spirit is built up.[1]

The Freudian Theory of Religion

If Marx dubbed religion as the opium of the masses, Freud dubbed it as "the universal obsessional neurosis of mankind".[2] Although to the extent that Freud focused his exercise on God it would not apply to Jainism, yet some aspects of his analysis can be brought into relation to Jainism.

The extreme asceticism of Jainism would appear, from a psychoanalytical point of view, to border on the pathological. In any case, whether Freudian approaches apply to Jainism or not, Jaina scholars have not hesitated to apply it to Hinduism, as, for instance, to the practice of *śrāddha*, referred to earlier.

> It is tempting to read Freudian symbolism into this belief system: the son, though perhaps desiring to "kill" his father (by preventing his rebirth), nevertheless performs his filial duty out of fear of "castration" (the loss of property and offspring). Perhaps more to the point, however, is the fact that in Indian society the parent seems fundamentally unwilling to relinquish his control over the son, to recognize the latter's adult status: through the institution of *śrāddha*, some semblance of parental control is maintained even in death. It would be interesting to investigate whether the Jainas, lacking the institutionalization of filial responsibility that *śrāddha* represents, have created some substitute ritual or social form which functions in an analogous manner.[3]

1. *Ibid.*, p. 234.
2. Cited, John H. Hick, *op. cit.*, p. 33.
3. Padmanabh S. Jaini, "Karma and the Problem of Rebirth", *op. cit.*, p. 234 note 38.

Challenge of Modren Science

The challenge of modern science has not been felt acutely by Jainism as by some other religions for two reasons: its preference for commonsense and its doctrine of the manysidedness of reality.

Science is rooted in common sense, although its subsequent development departs from many of our commonsensical notions and even contradicts them. But Jainism, on account of its adherence to common sense, shares science's caution in not being too quick to prefer the supernatural explanation over the natural. Thus Mahāvīra's "metaphysics was based on common-sense realism and intellectual reconciliation".[1] Similarly, the "Jaina logician is neither a sceptic nor an agnostic; but he is a realist working with sound common sense. He does not want to ignore the relative or conditional character of the judgement arising out of the very nature of the object of knowledge".[2]

1. A.N. Upadhye, *op. cit.*, p. 101.
2. *Ibid.*, p. 105.

CHAPTER IV

GOD, SUFFERING AND HUMAN BEINGS

I

According to Jainism, pain is more imminent than evil and more pervasive. A.L. Basham, before citing the following passage, from which "a very gory description of the pains of purgatory"[1] has been omitted, introduces it with the following final remark: "The reader should remember what we have said about the hylozoism of the Jains—the iron of the blacksmith's anvil is also in pain."[2] Now the passage:

All Creation Groans Together in Torment

From clubs and knives, stakes and maces, breaking my limbs,
An infinite number of times I have suffered without hope.
By keen-edged razors, by knives and shears,
Many times I have been drawn and quartered, torn apart and skinned.
Helpless in snares and traps, a deer,
I have been caught and bound and fastened, and often I have been killed.
A helpless fish, I have been caught with hooks and nets;
An infinite number of times I have been killed and scraped, split and gutted.
A bird, I have been caught by hawks or trapped in nets,
Or held fast by birdlime, and I have been killed an infinite number of times.
A tree, with axes and adzes by the carpenters

---

1. A.L. Basham, "The Basic Doctrines of Jainism", in Wm. Theodore de Bary, ed., *op. cit.*, Vol. I, p. 59-60.
2. *Ibid.*

An infinite number of times I have been struck and beaten
split and filed...
Ever afraid, trembling, in pain and suffering,
I have felt the utmost sorrow and agony...
In every kind of existence I have suffered
Pains which have scarcely known reprieve for a moment.[1]

In an atheistic system like Jainism, then, the problem is not so much evil as pain, a problem which has been portrayed so graphically in Jainism as to have led to its virtual identification with pessimism.[2]

This problem of pain is contextualized in Jainism, not with God's existence, but with existence itself. However, let us commence our study of the topic in the manner usual in text books of modern philosophy, which often make the following initial points:

(1) Evil refers to "physical pain, mental suffering and moral wickedness"[3] rather than to "that which is contrary to God's will".[4] That levels our playing field right there.

(2) Moral wickedness is a major contributor to physical pain and mental suffering.

(3) Natural suffering, however, exceeds human-induced suffering.[5]

II

In a Christian context the following points tend to be emphasized in this context: (1) that suffering is real and cannot be metaphysically brushed aside as illusory; (2) that it poses a dilemma in relation to God: "if God is perfectly loving, God must wish to abolish all evil; and if God is all-powerful, God must be able to abolish all evil. But evil exists; therefore God cannot be both omnipotent and perfectly loving"; (3) this dilemma has produced the following responses:

---

1. *Ibid.*, p. 59-60.
2. M. Hiriyanna, *The Essentials of Indian Philosophy*, p. 69. Also see Phyllis Granoff, "Jain Stories Inspiring Renunciation", in Donald S. Lopez, Jr., *op. cit.*, pp. 412-417.
3. John H. Hick, *op. cit.*, p. 39.
4. *Ibid.*
5. *Ibid.*

> There are three main Christian responses to the problem of evil: the Augustinian response, hinging upon the concept of the fall of man from an original state of righteousness; the Irenaean response, hinging upon the idea of the gradual creation of a perfected humanity through life in a highly imperfect world; and the response of modern process theology, hinging upon the idea of a God who is not all-powerful and not in fact able to prevent the evils arising either in human beings or in the processes of nature.[1]

Finally, there is a position common to all of these and this

> common ground is some form of what has come to be called the free-will defense, at least so far as the moral evil of human wickedness is concerned, for Christian thought has always seen moral evil as related the human freedom and responsibility. To be a person is to be a finite center of freedom, a (relatively) self-directing agent responsible for one's own decisions. This involves being free to act wrongly as well as rightly. There can therefore be no certainly in advance that a genuinely free moral agent will never choose amiss. Consequently, according to the strong form of free-will defense, the possibility of wrongdoing is logically inseparable from the creation of finite persons, and to say that God should not have created beings who might sin amounts to saying that God should not have created people.[2]

The points of convergence of these positions with a Jaina point of view may first be recognized. Curiously enough, these refer to the first and last points. As in Christianity, so also in Jainism, suffering is *real*, and is the outcome of the exercise of our free will. The chapter was introduced with a graphic recognition of its reality, so there is no need to pile up the agony. Our responsibility for it, however, calls for a fuller statement.

The dilemma of theism in relation to suffering is recognized by Jainism. It is, however, developed in a series of arguments which

1. *Ibid.*, p. 40.
2. *Ibid.*, p. 40.

logically connect the problem of God with the existence of suffering in the world, although *phenomenologically* Jainism emphasizes its existence in the world.

The Jaina argument proceeds from a concessive stance, that is, one which putatively concedes the existence of the creator. Now the question is asked: "'Why does he create the world' If he is said to be creating the world by his mere whim, no satisfactory explanation could be given to the law and order found in the universe. If he is said to be doing so for giving appropriate results to the adṛṣṭas or the merits and demerits accruing from the good and evil actions of the worldly beings, then it will have to be admitted that he is guided by something outside his being i.e. by the adṛṣṭas of the worldly beings. In that case, his activity will have to be regarded as subject to limitations—a contention which will go against his independence."[1] Let the whim be substituted by a motive—that too a benign one. Thus "It is held by some theists that Īśvara creates the world out of his mercy or *karuṇā* for the worldly beings. If it were so, the Jainas argue, there would have been only happiness in the world. But the world is so full of evil and pain that it cannot be looked upon as an act of divine mercy. If Īśvara creates the world out of mercy, why should he create, the Jainas ask, these evils and pains of life? Again, this world is so full of inequalities that one might bring a charge against Īśvara of maintaining favouritism in dealing with the worldly beings, as is evident from the fact that he makes some beings happy and others unhappy. This also goes against the view that Īśvara is merciful and that he creates the world out of mercy."[2] The Indian, like the Christian theist, might object that the suffering is not random but fine-tuned to acts of free will or karma. "In other words, all these pains and sufferings are to be traced to the moral responsibility of the beings, and not to the sweet will of God. But the Jainas ask: 'If this be so, what is it that Īśvara does'? If he cannot change the effects of *karma*, he is no Īśvara at all. Moreover, if all beings are led by their own *karmas* or adaṛṣṭas at every step, then *karma* or adṛṣṭa could very well account for the events of the world, and no

1. K.P. Sinha, *op. cit.*, p. 144-145.
2. *Ibid.*, p. 145.

God would be required for that purpose".[1] An extra argument is also thrown in to fix the cement: "Further, if Īśvara creates the world out of his mercy for the worldly beings, why should there be dissolution? It is held by some that Īśvara dissolves the world to give some relief to the worldly beings, and hence, dissolution is also an act of his mercy. But the Jainas argue that, the act of warding off evils after having created them is unwise; it were better if Īśvara did not create them at all."[2]

It is interesting to compare the fate of the free will argument in Christianity and Jainism. In Christianity it gets God off the hook. In Jainism it takes him down hook, line and sinker!

III

John Hick explicitly acknowledges that his discussion of the problem of evil is "confined to the problem of human suffering, the large and intractable problem of animal pain has not been taken up here."[3]

Jainism does not shy away from taking up the problem. Its contribution to the discussion of the problem might well be the frank inclusion of it in the discussion and of rendering it somewhat less intractable.

First of all, the Jainas provide us with a painstaking classification of the animal world, all animals being jīvas and thus susceptible to pain. "The Jains divide the jīvas according to the number of sense-organs they possess. The lowest class consists of plants, which possess only the sense-organ of touch. The next higher class is that of worms, which possess two senses of touch and taste. Next come the ants, etc., which possess touch, taste and smell. The next higher one that of bees, etc. possessing vision in addition to touch, taste and smell. The vertebrates possess all the five sense-organs. The higher animals among these, namely men, denizens of hell and the gods possess in addition to these an inner sense-organ namely *manas* by virtue of which they are called rational (samjñin) while the lower animals have to reason and are called asamjñin."[4]

1. *Ibid.*
2. *Ibid.*
3. John H. Hick, *op. cit.*, p. 47 note 11.
4. Surendranath Dasgupta, *op. cit.*, Vol. I, p. 191-192.

After the animals, even the so-called material world falls into the same category: "Proceeding towards the lowest animal we find that the Jainas regard all the four elements (earth, water, air, fire) as being animated by souls. Thus particles of earth, etc., are the bodies of souls called earth-lives, etc. These we may call elementary lives; they live and die and are born again in another elementary body. These elementary lives are either gross or subtle; in the latter case they are invisible."[1] We then move on to the next group within the same broad category. "The last class of one-organ lives are plants [mentioned earlier at the outset]. Of some plants each is the body of one soul only; but of other plants, each is an aggregation of embodied souls, which have all the functions of life such as respiration and nutrition in common. Plants in which only one soul is embodied are always gross, they exist in the habitable part of the world only. But those plants of which each is a colony of plant lives may *also* be subtle and invisible, and in that case they are distributed all over the world."[2] These *nigodas* are "colonial,[3] but they may also occupy the bodies of others and become "parasitic."[4] Gods, hell-beings and element bodies are spared this fate. On the other hand they tend to be concentrated in "certain roots and bulbs". In any case: "The whole universe is full of minute beings called *nigodas*; they are groups of infinite number of souls forming very small clusters, having respiration and nutrition in common and *experiencing extreme pains.* The whole space of the world is closely packed with them like a box filled with powder."[5]

IV

The Jaina solution to the problem of evil is ahiṁsā, generally translated as non-violence. The best one can do to remove suffering, first of all, is not to cause it. "Jainism is perhaps the only Indian religion which has explained the doctrine of ahiṁsā in a systematic

1. *Ibid.*, p. 190.
2. *Ibid.*
3. Padmanabh S. Jaini, *op. cit.*, p. 224.
4. Ibid.
5. Surendranath Dasgupta, *op. cit.*, Vol. I, p. 190, emphasis added. One might say that Jainism provides for the following birth categories (1) gods, (2) men, (3) animals and (4) "animals". The sum total of conceivable birth-situations (*yonis*) is placed at 8,400,000 [see Padmanabh S. Jaini, "Karma and the Problem of Rebirth in Jainism", *op. cit.*, p. 222, 228].

manner, because all other values were elaborated on this basis. Violence or injury is of three kinds: physical violence, which covers killing, wounding, and causing any physical pain; violence in words, which consists of using harsh language; and mental violence, which implies bearing ill feeling towards others."[1]

The concept has not only been explained most systematically[2] in Jainism, it has also been carried to its most extreme. Padmanabh S. Jaini thus points out: "we must be aware of one basic fact: the Jaina preoccupation with *ahiṁsā*, the avoidance of giving injury. Great importance has been attached to this concept by every Indian school, but none has carried it to the extreme of the Jainas. For them it is not simply the first among virtues by *the* virtue; all other restraints are simply elaborations of this central one."[3] Two further points are specially worth noting here. One is that while "*Hiṃsā* has ordinarily been understood in India as harm done to others; for Jainas, however, it refers primarily to injuring *oneself*—to behaviour which inhibits the soul's ability to attain *mokṣa*. Thus the killing of animals, for example, is reprehensible not only for the suffering produced in the victims, but even more so because it involves intense passions on the part of the killer, passions which bind him more firmly in the grip of saṃsāra. The Jaina concept of hiṃsā, then, is very broad in terms of the actions to which it

1. A.N. Upadhye, *op. cit.*, p. 106.
2. Consider the following description, for instance, of ahiṁsā in relation to the householder. "Further, violence may be committed, commissioned or consented to. A householder is unable to avoid all these forms of violence in an absolute manner, so he is expected to cause minimal injury to others. In view of the sort of society in which we have to live, injury is classified under four heads: first, there is *accidental* injury in the course of digging, pounding, cooking, and other such activities essential to daily living; second there is *occupational* injury, as when a soldier fights, an agriculturists tills the land, etc.; third there is *protective* injury, as when one protects one's own or other peoples's lives and honour against wild beasts and enemies; and last, there is intentional injury when one kills beings with the full intention of killing them, as in hunting or butchery. A householder is expected to abstain completely from *intentional* injury and as far as possible from the rest. It is the intention or the mental attitude that matters more than the act. So one has to take the utmost care to keep one's intentions pure and pious and to abstain from intentional injury. The practice of these various vows puts some restriction on the choice of a profession and makes for a humane outlook in society." (ibid.).
3. Padmanabh S. Jaini, *The Jaina Path of Purification*, p. 167.

refers; and the need for abandonment of such actions becomes of paramount importance to the spiritual aspirant".[1] The second point worth noting is that "Seen within this context, the forbidden substances mentioned above begin to show certain features in common. Most important is the fact that, in the Jaina view, partaking in any of these necessarily involves killing and so must be avoided. This fact is of course most obvious with regard to meat; thus it is not surprising that the taboo against eating animal flesh is enforced more strongly in the Jaina community than in any other. To perceive the violence supposedly inherent in partaking of the other prohibited foods, we must recall the Jaina belief in nigoda, the myriad single-sense creatures which inhabit almost every corner of the universe."[2] However, "While Jainas take very seriously the destruction of nigoda, it should be noted that violence against these creatures is considered far less terrible than that against higher animals. Thus a Jaina layman may on rare occasions consume medicinal preparations made with honey or wine, but under no circumstances may he take meat. If there is a single practice which can be called the hallmark of the Jaina, it must be this strict adherence to vegetarianism; his refusal to eat meat constitutes the most basic expression of his commitment to ahiṃsā."[3]

V

One might wish to ask at the end of all this: is there a Jaina theodicy?

In a sense, of course, there cannot be a Jaina theodicy because there is no God in relation to whom suffering and evil have to be explained. One should note, however, that "omniscience as defined by the Jainas, ...is clearly in the realm of the supramundane; indeed, one finds similar qualities ascribed to God by the theistic schools. Virtually no tradition other than Jainism has dared to attach so cosmic an attribute to a human being."[4] In the light of this it may well be asked how Jainism accounts for suffering.

1. *Ibid.*, p. 168.
2. *Ibid.*
3. *Ibid.* The extreme nature of Jaina commitment has been animadverted upon, see S. Radhakrishnan, *op. cit.*, Vol., p. 327-328.
4. Padmanabh S. Jaini, The Jaina Path of Purification, p. 266.

This question is best answered by first broadening the perspective from within which one might address it. Such an approach has been adopted by Nathmal Tatia. He writes:

> It will be helpful to begin with [Mahāvīra's] attitude towards life. A major part of Mahāvīra's teaching was concerned with the appeal not to interfere with the lives of others. Sorrow and suffering were as much the facts with Mahāvīra as with the Buddha. To get rid of the cycle of worldly existence was the common end of both of them as of the Upanisadic thinkers. The Buddha found everything impermanent and hence sorrowful and substanceless. But Mahāvīra's attitude was not so radical. If the Upanisadic thinkers found the immutable reality behind the world of phenomena and plurality, and the Buddha denounced everything as fleeting and sorrowful and pointed to the futility of all speculation, Mahāvīra adhered to the common experience, found no contradiction between permanence and change and was free from all absolutism. Existence is not an evil by itself and so freedom does not mean total cessation of it.[1]

This statement contains part of the answer, the rest of it is contained in what follows:

> With Upanisadic thinkers what is impermanent is sorrowful and only empirical. The reality therefore is what is permanent and blissful. With the Buddha also everything is impermanent and hence sorrowful and substanceless. Freedom, therefore, means total cessation. But Mahāvīra did not believe in absolute permanence or total cessation. If life were accepted as an illusory phenomenon, or if it were accepted as nothing but evil and suffering, absolute permanence or total cessation would be the truth or the desired goal. But with Mahāvīra change was as much real as permanence, and so his position was quite distinct from those of the absolutists. Freedom means freedom from passions only. It is a qualitative change rather than total cessation.[2]

1. Nathmal Tatia, *op. cit.*, p. 17-18, emphasis added.
2. *Ibid.*, p. 18, emphasis added.

CHAPTER V

REVELATION, FAITH AND KNOWLEDGE

I

John Hick writes, after surveying the arguments for and against the existence of God: "It seems, then, that the universe is religiously ambiguous—capable of being construed both religiously and naturalistically. This is tacitly acknowledged by the traditional term used for human awareness of God, namely faith, as distinguished from knowledge".[1] John Hick then takes up the concept of faith, and the correlative concept of revelation, for examination.

Faith and Knowledge

Faith, and the discussion of faith, plays a major role in the philosophy of religion. This feature of the modern philosophy of religion may be attributed to its Christian setting. In Christianity, salvation is a post-mortem state. Faith, therefore, involves faith in "things unseen" because things cannot be seen—as they are said to be—while one is still alive. They can only be seen 'through a glass, darkly'. By contrast, the Jaina context is very different. In Jainism, salvation, in principle, can be achieved here and now. Faith, therefore, is not as important a category, and certainly not as important as knowledge. It is not that faith has no role to play in Jainism at all, rather it has a very different role to play.

The fact of the matter is that knowledge plays the role in Jainism which is often assigned to faith in Christianity, and in the Western philosophy of religion. This becomes apparent when the voluntarist theories of faith in the Western philosophy of religion are interrogated from a Jaina point of view.

---

1. John H. Hick, *op. cit.*, p. 56.

Pascal's View of Faith

Pascal's views on faith may be presented in two steps. The first step emphasized the *rationality* of faith. The point at issue is: does God exist or not? Now, he says, "If we wager our lives that God exists, we stand to gain eternal salvation if we are right and to lose little if we are wrong. If, on the other hand, we wager our lives that there is no God, we stand to gain little if we are right but to lose eternal happiness if we are wrong... If you gain you gain all; if you lose, you lose nothing. Wager, then without hesitation that He is".[1] As John Hick notes, Pascal's famous wager "amounts to a rational form of self-insurance".[2]

The second step emphasizes the *possibility* of faith. Pascal believed that faith could be generated in steps, in one who did not have it to begin with:

> You would like to attain faith, and do not know the way; you would like to cure yourself of unbelief, and ask the remedy for it. Learn of those who have been bound like you...Follow the way by which they began; by acting as if they believed, taking the holy water, having masses said, etc. Even this will naturally make you believe, and deaden your acuteness.[3]

Or in the jargon of modern pop psychology: "fake it till you make it". This statement is not meant to trivialize Pascal's position, which, as we shall see later, resembles some aspects of Jainism, as we take more serious aim.

On the whole, however, Pascal's position is difficult to support from within Jainism. First of all, it can be applied to Jainism itself. Accept Jainism and you might become liberated in this very life if it is true; if is not true, the status quo continues. Of course, if Jainism is false and Christianity is true, then you have a lot to lose, as Mrs. Sinclair Stevenson would seem to argue[4], but that begs the

1. Cited, *ibid.*, p. 59.
2. *Ibid.*
3. Cited, *ibid*, p. 59.
4. Mrs. Sinclair Stevenson, *The Heart of Jainism* (London: Oxford University Press, 1915) passim, especially pp. 297-298. Sometimes her treatment of certain aspects of Jainism has even distressed non-Jainas, see Mm. P.E. Gopinath Kaviraj's introduction to Koshelya Walli, *op. cit.*, p. 1 note 1.

whole question. Next, from a Jaina point of view, one has a lot to lose if one worships a God who does not exist. Such a belief is one of the three darts (*Śalya*) which ruin Right Conduct:

> A second poisonous dart is false belief or Mithyātva Śalya, which consists in holding a false god to be a true one, a false guru to be a true guru, and a false religion to be a true religion; by so doing one absolutely injures Right Knowledge and Right Faith which lead to Right Conduct; this is therefore a highly poisonous dart. The great evil wrong belief does shows how supremely important it is for men to know who is the true Tīrthankara, and the definition, which the Jaina repeat every day at their devotions, runs as follows:
>
> 'He who is omniscient, free from all love of the world and from all failings; he who is worshipped by the three worlds and who explains the inner meaning [of religion] as it exists: this adorable deity is the great god.'
>
> The Jaina similarly define a false god:
>
> 'Those gods who retain women, weapons and rosaries, who are steeped in attachment and so stained, who are in the habit of giving and accepting favours, these can give no help towards deliverance.'[1]

Finally, to try to generate faith in such a false God would only compound the original error. However, the idea that a state of spiritual exaltation could be reached by stages—the way one might attain faith—is accepted in Jainism, and finds expression in its doctrine of gunastānas or stages of spiritual development.[2]

William James' View of Faith

According to William James, the issue of the existence or nonexistence of God is so momentous that one has to choose. He writes:

> We cannot escape the issue by remaining skeptical and waiting for more light, because, although we do avoid error

1. Mrs. Sinclair Stevenson, *op. cit.*, p. 246. The last citation is an apparent dig at some of the Hindu gods. One wonders how Christ, who grants the favour of deliverance by dying a gory death on the Cross, will go down with non-violent Jainas.
2. K.P. Sinha, *op. cit.*, p. 114-116.

> in that way *if religion be untrue*, we lose the good, *if it be true*, just as certainly as if we positively chose to disbelieve. *Better risk loss of truth than chance of error* – that is your faith–vetoer's exact position. He is actively playing his stake as much as the believer is; he is backing the field against the religious hypothesis, just as the believer is backing the religious hypothesis against the field. To preach scepticism to us as a duty until "sufficient evidence" for religion be found, is tantamount therefore to telling us, when in presence of the religious hypothesis, that to yield to our fear of its being error is wiser and better than to yield to our hope that it may be true...Dupery for dupery, what proof is there that dupery through hope is so much worse than dupery through fear? I, for one, can see no proof; and I simply refuse obedience to the scientist's command to imitate his kind of option, in a case where my own stake is important enough to give me the right to choose my own form of risk.[1]

Two points strike one's attention immediately. First of all, William James' position seems to be essentially similar to Pascal's, the difference lying in the fact that Pascal emphasizes its *rationality* and William James its *gravity*. But the views of both—and this is the second point—are tilted *towards* theism, however philosophical the idiom in which they are expressed. In fact, the position of William James, like that of Pascal, can also be stated in two steps. Just as, in the second stage, Pascal recommended the cultivation of faith; William James recommends that we cultivate God; but if we first insist of a proof thereof such cultivation is not possible:

> ... just as a man who in a company of gentlemen made no advances, asked a warrant for every concession, and believed no one's word without proof, would cut himself off by such churlishness from all the social rewards that a more trustworthy spirit would earn—so here, one who would shut himself up in snarling logicality and try to make the gods extort his recognition willynilly, or not get it at all, might cut himself off forever from his only opportunity of making the gods' acquaintance.[2]

On account of the similarity between their stances, the Jaina criticisms of Pascal's position, *pari passu*, also apply to that of William James.

It is also helpful to consider the criticism of William James by John Hick in a Jaina light. According to John Hick the "basic weakness of James' position is that it constitutes an unrestricted license for wishful thinking".[1] He considers William James' rejection of the Mahdi as the Messiah, on the ground that it does not appear as a "live option" in James' mind, unconvincing. It only shows that the option "did not conform to the assumptions controlling his thinking" and seemed to have little to do with "the truth or falsity of the Mahdi's assertions", which should certainly concern us. It is the way value has become disengaged from fact in William James' position which worries John Hick and makes him conclude that "if our aim is to believe what is *true*, and not necessarily what we like, James' universal permissiveness will not help us".[2]

John Hick's critique of William James has been presented at some length because it resembles a criticism often voiced *against* Jainism. Just as John Hick accuses William James of *axiological* permissiveness, Hindu thinkers have often accused Jaina thought of an *ontological* permissiveness, on account of its doctrine of the manifoldness of reality. "Jainism makes basic and fundamental the principle that truth is relative to our standpoint. The general character of reality is given in several partial views" and the temptation to hang on to the part we hold may be too strong to overcome, thereby allowing us to believe in anything we like. The defence of William James may be left to others[3] but it might be worthwhile here to note that, so far as the Jaina position is concerned, Jaina philosophy is quite concerned with distinguishing genuine, if variant, standpoints from pseudo-standpoints.[4]

F.R. Tennant's View of Faith

The next scholar whose views on faith may be usefully examined

1. *Ibid.*, p. 60.
2. *Ibid.*
3. See John H. Hick, *op. cit.*, p. 60 note 13.
4. B.K. Matilal, *op. cit.*, p. 8, 44, 45, 46, etc.

is F.R. Tennant. Crucial to Tennant's position is the distinction between belief and faith. In a passage, often cited, he writes:

> Belief is more or less constrained by fact or Actuality that already is or will be, independently of any striving of ours, and which convinces us. Faith, on the other hand, reaches beyond the Actual or the given to the ideally possible, which in the first instance it creates, as the mathematician posits his entities, and then by practical activity may realize or bring into Actuality. Every machine of human invention has thus come to be. Again, faith may similarly lead to knowledge of Actuality which it in no sense creates, but which would have continued, in absence of the faith-venture, to be unknown: as in the discovery of America by Columbus.[1]

The difference between science and religion, rests, for Tennant, on (1) faith and (2) its intellectual context. Tennant goes on to connect, broadly, one kind of faith with the quantitative, the "how" aspect of things and thus with science, and another kind of faith with the qualitative, the "why" aspect of things and with religion. "Science postulates what is requisite to make the world amenable to the kind of thought that conceives of the structure of the universe, and its orderedness according to quantitative law; theology, and sciences of valuation, postulate what is requisite to make the world amenable to the kind of thought that conceives of the why and wherefore, the meaning or purpose of the universe, and its orderedness according to teleological principles".[2]

Note what he does *not* say: that what can be resolved by discovery and experiment qualifies as belief and characterises science; the kind of doubt which is beyond empirical resolution calls for faith and characterises religion.

John Hick thinks that the use of the same word faith, both in a scientific and a religious context, makes for obfuscation, for the essential nature of the two faiths is very different—one impels towards verification here and now, and the other points to the

1. Cited in John H. Hick, *op. cit.*, p. 61.
2. Cited, *ibid.*

hereafter. Tennant attempts to see faith, according to John Hick, in "numerous examples of the gaining of material and moral advantages, the surmounting of trials and afflictions, and the attainment of heroic life, by men of old who were inspired by faith. It is thus that faith is pragmatically 'verified' and that certitude as to the unseen is established". John Hick finds this attempt misleading. Tennant, who often uses the words "faith" and "belief" interchangeably, is even prepared to say: "There are instances in which a belief that is not true, in the sense of corresponding with fact, may inspire one with lofty ideals and stimulate one to strive to be a more worthy person".[1] As John Hick pointedly observes: This admission reduces religious faith, as Tennant conceives it, to an unverifiable hope, and thereby undermines his attempt to "assimilate religious to scientific cognition".[2]

From a Jaina point of view, two observations could be made regarding the foregoing discussion. The first is that the arrow of Jain thinking in general moves in the opposite direction–from knowledge to faith rather than vice versa. Thus, as Mrs. Sinclair Stevenson notes: "Mahāvīra, himself said: 'First knowledge and then mercy', unless a man know what a jīva is, how can he show mercy to him?"[3] The second is that truth and faith can be brought in closer relation in Jainism on account of its realism, pragmatism and provision of pre-mortem liberation.

> Central among the Three Jewels is Right Faith; for unless one believes in what one knows, how will one follow it? Samyak Darśana stands for true faith and insight into the great Jaina doctrines and scriptures. The Jaina say that it is like the digit I, which, standing before the ciphers that follow it, gives them value, for without faith all conduct is worthless.
>
> 'To hold the truth as truth, and untruth as untruth, this is true faith.'[4]

Paul Tillich's View of Faith

Paul Tillich famously said that "Faith is the state of being ultimately

1. Cited, *ibid.*, p. 62
2. *Ibid.*
3. Mrs, Sinclair Stevenson, *op. cit.*, p. 245.
4. *Ibid.*

concerned"[1] and when pressed to clarify whether by that he meant the *attitude* of concern or the *object* of that attitude,[2] resolved the issue by identifying the two: "the ultimate of the act of faith and the ultimate that is meant in the act of faith are one and the same",[3] thereby dissolving the subject-object dichotomy.[4]

Analogous to the Tillichian thinking about faith is the Jaina thinking about knowledge–given the different epistemic priorities of theism and Jainism. In the Jaina case, the consciousness of the *jīva* "reveals its own nature as well as that of the object. Jñeya or the object of knowledge includes self and not self. As light reveals itself and other objects, even so does Jñāna reveal itself and others".[5] Thus the argument develops in the opposite direction and holds even in the state of perfect knowledge or kevalajñāna.

The Propositional View of Revelation and Faith

These various views of faith also imply a particular view of revelation in the Western philosophy of religion. It is known as the propositional view of revelation. According to this view, God has revealed certain propositional truths to humanity through the Bible. This propositional view of revelation, from the point of view of current discussion, includes two key ideas: (1) that "the religious person who appeals to revelation is referring to theological propositions that God is supposed to have delivered to humankind" and (2) the person is ready to believe the propositions on "insufficient evidence".[6]

The Jaina view of revelation and faith, by analogy, would read as follows: (1) that omniscient beings called *jinas* or *siddhas* have revealed the nature of the universe and our place in it and (2) the acceptance of their teachings involves following a path which leads to deliverance, an attainment possible in this very life.

1. Cited, John H. Hick, *op. cit.*, p. 62.
2. *Ibid.*
3. *Ibid.*, p. 63.
4. *Ibid.*
5. S. Radhakrishnan, *op. cit.*, Vol. I, p. 297. For a fuller exposition see Nathmal Tatia, *Studies in Jaina Philosophy* (Banaras: Jain Cultural Research Society, 1951) p. 185 and 186.
6. John H. Hick, *op. cit.*, p. 58.

It is a matter of some interest that despite the theistic and non-theistic orientations of the two views of revelation and the obvious differences, there are some interesting points of convergence. (1) In both the systems the revealed teachings derive their validity not from the *texts* themselves, as in some forms of Hinduism, but from their source—God or Jina. This point is of particular interest in the case of Jainism for two reasons: (1) its two major branches the Digambara (sky-clad) and the Śvetāmbara (white-clad) differ among themselves considerably regarding its 'canon'; and (2) despite the fact that "the Jaina scriptures are comparatively late in their final form, there is so little divergence in fundamentals between the two great Jaina sects that it seems that the basic teachings of both are very ancient indeed and are essentially those of Mahāvīra himself."[1]

This state of affairs raises at least four points of interest for the philosophy of religion. It now seems possible to distinguish between the texts (oral or written) of a religion, and its teachings. It is possible to entertain four possibilities in this respect: (1) that the texts may be in a state of confusion and yet the teachings can be found in a state of pristine preservation; (2) that both the texts and its teachings be in a state of coherent preservation; (3) that the texts may be in a singular state of preservation but their interpretations may be singularly divergent and (4) that both the texts as well as the teachings be in a state of considerable variance. I hope I am not being unfair in proposing that Buddhism provides an illustration of the fourth option; Hinduism (and perhaps Christianity) of the third; Islam of the second and Jainism of the first.

Now I can come to the main point for the sake of which the exercise was undertaken, namely, that *but for Jainism*, philosophers of religion may not even have felt disposed to entertain the first possibility as credible. Jainism illustrates the paradoxical possibility that it is possible for revealed propositions to survive in an orderly fashion without a revealed text to go with them. Should we then not dignify such a case with the description of *philosophical revelation*, as distinguished from a religious one?

1. A.L. Basham, *The Wonder That Was India* (London: Sidgwick & Jackson, 1988) p. 290.

Be that as it may, if Jainism may be said to represent a special case of the propositional view of revelation, then in another sense it may be said to present a unique case of it. Given the Jaina belief in the manifoldness of reality, it follows that what we have here is a *multipropositional view of revelation.* The technical expression used within Jainism for this position is Anekāntavāda. It was explained earlier but the explanation is cited again for ready reference.

> The principle of anekānta can be briefly described as the acceptance of the manifoldness of reality. Jaina philosophers claim that no philosophic or metaphysical proposition can be true if it is simply asserted without any condition or limitation. If a proposition is asserted as "x is f" then it becomes *ekānta* 'one-sided.' This means that the proposition ascribes *unconditionally* a predicate-property to the subject and thereby excludes other rival possibilities (contradictory predicates). For Jainism such an unconditional assertion violates the principle of *anekānta.* As far as the Jainas are concerned, if a metaphysical proposition violates this principle, it is to be regarded as false.[1]

This doctrine has implications for virtually every aspect of the philosophy of religion. If we confine our remarks to the theme on hand, it is clear that a system which allows for multiple propositional statements about the nature of reality through its revealed scriptures represents an unprecedented approach to the whole issue of revelation and faith.

There is a parallel of sorts, however, between the Christian propositional view of revelation, according to which God guarantees the truth of revelation and the Jaina view, in which the same is guaranteed by the omniscience of the teacher. Thus the "authority of the Jaina teachings rests ultimately on the fact that they were preached by an omniscient being; thus they are every bit as unverifiable and dogmatic as those accepted by an orthodox Hindu or Christian. Nevertheless, Jaina teachers claim that only the teachings of the Jina can stand the scrutiny of reason; they further

1. B.K. Matilal, *op. cit.*, p. 2.

contend that in comparison with other religions (for example, Vaiṣṇavism or Śaivism) Jaina doctrines are most consistent with the actual conduct demanded of the faithful".[1] The propositional character is further confirmed by the fact that "The Jaina tradition is unanimous in affirming that the great pontiff Bhadrabāhu (circa 360 B.C.) was the last person who knew all fourteen Pūrvas by heart. After him, knowledge of the Pūrvas was lost; most of those mendicants who had memorized portions thereof perished in the great Magadha famine".[2]

A Non-propositional View of Revelation and Faith

It is now time to recognise that "Christian thought contains two very different understandings of the nature of revelation and, as a result, two different conceptions of faith (as the human reception of revelation), of the Bible (as a medium of revelation), and of theology (as discourse based upon revelation)."[3] We have so far confined our attention to only one of them, namely, the view that "the content of revelation is a body of truths expressed in statements or propositions",[4] that "revelation is the imparting to people of divinely authenticated truths".[5] From this point of view: "Revelation may be defined as the communication of some truth by God to rational creatures through means which are beyond the ordinary course of nature".[6]

We now turn to the consideration of a different view of revelation. It is known as the nonpropositional (or the *Heilsgeschichtliche*) view, according to which "the content of revelation is not a body of truths about God, but God coming within the orbit of human experience by acting in history. From this point of view, theological propositions, as such are not revealed but represent human attempts to understand the significance of revelatory events. This nonpropositional conception of revelation is connected with the modern renewed emphasis upon the *personal* character of God and

1. Padmanabha S. Jaini, *The Jaina Path of Purification*, p. 89.
2. *Ibid.*; p. 50.
3. John H. Hick, *op. cit.*, p. 56.
4. *Ibid.*
5. *Ibid.*
6. *The Catholic Encyclopedia*, cited, *ibid.*

the thought that the divine-human personal relationship consists of something more than the promulgation and reception of theological truths".[1]

This view runs into some obstacles when an attempt is made to extend it to Jainism. On the face of it, this should not be so, for Jainism can be traced back to a historical Mahāvīra, just as Christianity can be traced back to Jesus. Further reflection reveals another parallel: just as Jesus was preceded by a number of prophets, so was Mahāvīra. According to the Jaina tradition, there have been twenty-three such forerunners (including one, Malli[2], whose gender is disputed by its two sects). Mahāvīra appears as the last in the list.

After a point, however, the parallels can mislead. For one, although Mahāvīra is sometimes represented as reforming the legacy of the preceding *tīrthankara,* Pārśva by name, typically the *tīrthankara's* are depicted as conveying the same message, and not fulfilling, in a Christian sense, the earlier prophets. The perspective which is brought to bear on the succession of the *tirthankaras* thus is rather different. *"According to the belief of the orthodox Jains, the Jaina religion is eternal, and it has been revealed again and again in every one of the endless succeeding periods of the world by innumerable Tīrthankaras.* In the present period the first Tīrthankara was Ṛṣabha and the last, the 24th, was Vardhamāna Mahāvīra. All Tīrthankaras have reached moksa at their death, and they neither care for nor have any influence on worldly affairs; but yet they are regarded as 'Gods' by the Jains and are worshipped".[3]

One final point also needs to be considered. While the Christian revelation deals with the entry of God into the world as the revelatory event, for the Jaina prophets their own experience of the world itself was the revelatory experience *par excellence.* The Christian nonpropositional view is formulated somewhat at the *cost* of our common-sense experience and interpretation of the world, the Jaina view is *based* on it. Mahāvīra, it is said, "did not fall into the trap of abstract logic [or divine intervention] because he did not

1. *Ibid.*, p. 64.
2. Vasudha Narayanan, *op. cit.*, p. 144.
3. Surendranath Dasgupta, *op. cit.*, Vol. I, p. 168-169.

depreciate common-sense interpretation of experience. The logical attitude of Mahāvīra is intimately bound up with his empiricism".[1]

A Non-propositional View of Revelation and Faith: Another Perspective

Jainism raises some intriguing questions for the traditional philosopher of religion. An obvious one is the fact that "Its contribution to the Indian heritage is more significant than might be expected from its numerical strength".[2] One is tempted to say that, in this respect, Jainism has been for Indian civilization, what Judaism has been for Western civilization. Yet another challenging feature consists of the fact that the "fundamental philosophical positions of Jainism have remained the same" without a safeguarded scripture,[3] "unlike those of Buddhism which went on changing from school to school",[4] schools which incidentally, in Jainism, like Buddhism itself, are not mentioned in the Jaina canon at all.[5]

One of the points of dispute between the two Jaina sects, the Digambara and the Śvetāmbara, as mentioned earlier, is the canon. It is in the context of this controversy that *code of conduct* emerges virtually as a form of non-propositional revelation. For "In their displeasure over certain portions of the codified canonical recension of Pātaliputra, [the Digambara] probably rejected so much material as to leave themselves with virtually no canon whatsoever. This explanation also fits well with the Digambaras' extreme emphasis *upon aspects of practice* (especially nudity) *rather than literature,* for in the absence of ancient scripture it was finally only the code of conduct of their sect which could define it as a unique and individual entity".[6]

1. Nathmal Tatia, *op. cit.*, p. 27. The extreme Jain commitment to non-violence, however, has been criticised from the point of view of common sense (see S. Radhakrishnan, *op. cit.*, Vol. I, p. 327-329.
2. A.N. Upadhye, *op. cit.*, p. 100.
3. Kendall W. Folkert, *Scripture and Community: Collected Essays on the Jains* (edited by John E. Cort) (Atlanta, Georgia: Scholars Press, 1993) p. 88, and Chapter 6, passim.
4. *Ibid.*, p. 102.
5. Padmanabha S. Jaini, *The Jaina Path of Purification,* p. 10.
6. *Ibid.*, p. 25, emphasis added.

From another point of view, however, the Jaina canon as a whole—represents a case of pristine propositional revelation. Padmanabha S. Jaini remarks: "Earlier, the Jaina belief that the sermons of a Jina take the form known as divyadhvani, the divine sound, was alluded to. It is said, moreover, that this sound manifests *artha*, the meaning or import of a Jina's teachings. Artha is in turn translated into sūtra, the canonical scriptures, by the several gāṇadharas or chief disciples; these gāṇadharas must have taken their mendicant vows in the presence of the Jina and must be endowed with such purity as to attain nirvāna in that very life. All Jainas accept the fact that their scriptures originated in this way. There is sectarian disagreement, however, over the precise nature of the events involved. Whereas Digambaras imagine the divyadhvani as a monotone—like the sound of *om*—which only the gaṇadharas are able to comprehend, Śvetāmbaras suggest that the Jina speaks in a human language that is divine in the sense that men of all regions, and animals, can benefit from hearing it. In the latter interpretation, the role of the gaṇadharas would be less one of translation than simply of compiling and organizing the Jina's words into a comprehensive and systematic body of teachings".[1]

Thus in the present context, the Digambaras incline more towards a sonoral propositional view of revelation.

Jaina Perspective on Faith

Like a magician saving his final trick for the last, we must now deal with the fact that *faith* is one of the three jewels (*ratnatraya*) of Jainism. The three jewels are usually cited as "true insight (*samyak-darśana*) right knowledge (*samyak-jñāna*) and proper conduct (*samyak-cāritra*)",[2] but the first one is also rendered as 'right faith'. Jainism also uses the word *pūjā* in the context of adoration of Jaina figures, which means worship in its usual connotation.[3]

Both these usages, however, have to be understood carefully. The point regarding faith may be clarified in three steps. The first

1. *Ibid.*, p. 42-43. Also see Vasudha Narayanan, *op. cit.*, p. 147.
2. Padmanabha S. Jaini, *The Jaina Path of Purification*, p. 200.
3. But see K.C. Sogani, "Jaina Faith and Morals", in G.S. Talib, ed., *Jainism* (Patiala: Punjabi University, 1975) p. 58.

step would consist of the recognition of the existential situation in which initially all of us find ourselves, even as budding philosophers of religion.

> While every Indian doctrinal system stresses the importance of perception and reasoning in validating its position on a given issue, it is nevertheless true that certain fundamental problems—for example, the nature of death, the possibility of salvation, the operational laws of the universe —are simply not subject to the direct or rational approach. Speculations concerning these problems must, if they are to be accepted, become objects of faith..[1]

Such faith might be called, for want of a better word, *preparatory faith for the spiritual journey.*

> According to the Jainas, one who has not attained samyak-darsana is likely to fall prey to nihilism or skepticism, refusing to believe in the existence of anything which he has not seen with his own eyes, as it were. If he is prone to the desire for heavens or supernatural boons, on the other hand, he may develop a dogmatic, blind faith in theories propounded by one or another of the "one-sided" (ekāntavādin) religious systems. The experience of true insight is said to save a person from drifting into these wrong views.[2]

It is, however, cautiously transformed into preparatory faith for the *Jaina spiritual journey.* in due course.

> While Jainas do not claim that samyak-darśana brings answers to *all* the great mysteries of existence, they do hold that it generates an important quality called *āstikya,* affirmation; this in turn becomes the basis for the "educated faith" (*śraddhā*) of the Jaina. Specifically, one who possesses *āstikya*

1. *Ibid.,* p. 150.
2. *Ibid.*

> will manifest a firm belief in the reality of nine things (*tattva*): the sentient (*jāva*), the insentient (*ajīva*), karmic influx (*āsrava*), unwholesome karmas (*pāpa*), wholesome karmas (*punya*), bondage (*bandha*), stoppage of karmic influx (*samvara*), dissociation of bound karmas (*nirjarā*), and liberation (*mokṣa*). Accepting the existence of these nine is the final behavioral "mark" of having attained samyak-darśana; thus we may understand the famous Jaina sūtra which says: *tattvārtha-śraddhānam samyak-darśanam*: "True insight is faith in the tattvas."[1]

The point which seems to emerge is that the difference between Christian and Jaina faith is not so much in the *nature* but rather in the object and *role* of faith. This point is reinforced when Jaina worship is compared with Hindu theistic worship. "The Jinas take the *place* of Hindu gods, but do not play a similar *role* in the Jaina ritual; they are seen as noble examples of the highest state to which man can aspire, and never as istadevatā, the personal deity with whom one can enter into an intimate relationship".[2]

Two factors radically affect the operation of faith in Jainism: (1) its non-theistic orientation and (2) the provision of pre-mortem salvation. The former gives faith an intellectual[3] rather than an emotional flavour and the latter makes faith an enabling rather than a final cause.

1. *Ibid.*, p. 151.
2. *Ibid.*, p. 295.
3. See Nathmal Tatia, *op. cit.*, p. 148.

CHAPTER VI

EPISTEMOLOGY AND ONTOLOGY

After a survey of the arguments for or against the existence of God, and after examining the tantalizing possibility that the questions thus raised may be ambiguous but still not unanswerable through revelation and faith, John Hick is led to conclude: "In spite of the immense intellectual investment that has gone into the various attempts to demonstrate the existence of God, the conclusion that this is indemonstrable agrees not only with the contemporary philosophical understanding of the nature and limits of logical proof but also with the biblical understanding of our knowledge of God".[1] And we might add: with our understanding of Jaina philosophy. The question then arises: are we looking at a dead end? Have we run into the limits of proof?

Limits of Proof

It might be useful, at this stage, to pause for a moment and to summarize the main routes Western philosophy has taken in tackling the issues which arise in a philosophy of religion. John Hick offers the following summation for our benefit: "Philosophy recognizes two ways in which human beings may come to know whatever there is to be known. One way (stressed by empiricism) is through experience, and the other (stressed by rationalism) is through reasoning. The limitation of the rationalist way is that the only truths capable of being strictly proved are analytic and ultimately tautological. We cannot by logic alone demonstrate any matters of fact and existence; these must be known through experience".[2] Hick continues:

1. John H. Hick, *op. cit.*, p. 68.
2. *Ibid.*

> That two and two equal four can be certified by strict proof; but that we live in world of objects in space, and that there is this table and that oak tree and those people, are facts that could never be known independently of sense perception. If nothing were given through experience in its various modes, we should never have anything to reason about. This is as true in religion as in other fields. If God exists, God is not an idea but a reality outside us; in order to be known to men and women, God must therefore become manifest in some way within their experience.[1]

The Jaina response would emphasize the fact that reason and experience; culture and nature; and other such dualities are all capable of being transformed into dualisms, which in course of time become antagonistic, with one mode of philosophical explanation trying to gain ascendancy over the other, *overlooking* the fact that both are equally given in our encounter with the world. This is what the Jaina philosopher means when he says that our thought is relative, that is, relative to one or the other. "The whole reality in its completeness cannot be grasped by this partial thought or expression. Nor can it be comprehended by combining these thoughts or expressions. What is required is the radical change in our absolutistic attitude. The error lies with the attitude and not with the thought or expression. Attachment and repulsion are the two great enemies of philosophical thinking. A thinker should not be guided by abstractionist tendencies which are responsible for mutually contradictory systems of thought. These tendencies are born of predilections, more or less inherent. It is as much difficult to get rid of these predilections as to be rid of the other evils of life. Truth reveals itself to an impartial thinker".[2] In the present context this would mean a thinker partial neither to rationalism nor empiricism.

This is where the need for a historical explanation becomes important. I am using the word *historical* here in a special sense—to refer to how Jainism arose in an intellectual environment in

1. *Ibid.*, p. 68-69.
2. Nathmal Tatia, *op. cit.*, p. 22.

which both rationalism and empiricism flourished in India in their Indian versions. Thus empiricism was present, in its cruder forms, in the materialism of Ajita Keśakambalī and the atomism of Pakdha Kacchāyana, while rationalism can be traced in the Upanisadic speculations. In a sense, empiricism, in its sophisticated version, is also found in Buddhism. Rationalism also finds its expression in Vedānta. Now *both* at the time when it arose, and its later history, Jainism has tried to take a position between these two intellectual streams, not in an exclusive but inclusive way. It takes recourse, therefore, both to logical empiricism and logical rationalism. As an example of logical empiricism we may cite its critique of *avidyā* or ignorance in Indian thought. In most schools it becomes an abstract entity. However,

> We have found that *mithyātva* or mithyādarśana (perverted attitude) is the Jain equivalent of *avidyā quâ* the fundamental or basic defect responsible for worldly existence. *Avidyā quâ* the conditions of worldly existence consists in the threefold elements of perverted attitude, perverted cognition (*mythyājñāna*) and perverted conduct (*mithyācāritra*). The Jaina philosopher does not agree with those who regard perverted cognition alone as the condition of worldly existence. Perverted cognition is only an effect of perverted attitude (*mithyātva*) which is the most fundamental condition of worldly existence. We shall have occasions in the chapters that follow for further elucidation of the conceptions of the nature of this 'perverted attitude'.
>
> The conception of the nature of *avidyā* depends upon the conception of the nature of reality. It is because of this that we have been led to criticise the various conceptions of reality of the different systems of thought while recording the Jain philosopher's objections against the different conceptions of *avidyā. We have shown the Jaina's credence in logical empiricism which regards logic without experience blind and experience without logic a cripple.*[1]

Jainism resorts to logical rationalism when answering the question of the relation of such perversity (*avidyā*) to the soul.

1. Nathmal Tatia, *op. cit.*, p. 218-219, emphasis added.

> In one sense, the question is as absurd as the question 'Why should the self exist?' The existence of the self is an ultimate fact and the existence of delusion coeval with it is equally an ultimate fact to which no question of origination can be relevant. The mithyātva is there, and it is not that we do not know its nature. Its nature and functions are well known. We also know its conditions. We do not know the beginning because it has no beginning. Why should we hesitate to accept a fact if our experience does not contradict it? The Jaina attitude is too realistic to abandon the verdict of experience, to speculate about possible answers to such ultimate issues, and as a result to adjust or compromise the facts of common experience. The Jaina philosophers, in matters of logical thinking, strictly follow the verdict of experience and do not surrender experience to abstract reasoning. The mithyātva, therefore, is accepted as beginningless on the basis of uncontradicted experience and also because no beginning can be postulated without self-contradiction.[1]

So far we have taken two historical considerations into account. A third point could also be introduced at this stage. It has been said that "rationalist assumptions... have dominated much of Western philosophy since the time of Descartes. Descartes held that we can properly be said to know only those truths that are self-evident or can be reached by logical inferences from self-evident premises. The still popular idea that to know means to be able to prove is a legacy of this tradition".[2] After observing thus, John Hick notes that it is in "the present century, under the influence of G.E. Moore (1873-1958) and others, the view gained ground that Cartesian doubt, far from being the most rational of procedures, is actually perverse and irrational. It is, Moore protested, absurd to think that we need to prove the existence of a world in which we are living".[3] It is difficult to imagine a Jaina thinker not concurring with this view.

1. *Ibid.* p. 146.
2. John H. Hick, *op. cit.*, p. 69.
3. *Ibid.*, p. 69.

Self-Evident Nature of Existence

In a certain sense Jainism and Sāmkhya, despite their philosophical differences,[1] represent this common-sensical belief in Indian thought. The materialists assert the ultimate existence of matter alone and the idealists, only of consciousness. But it is obvious to all that our normal experience of life discloses the simultaneous presence of *both.* We experience material objects, as well as immaterial states of consciousness, and a system of thought willing to assign reality and significance to both should hold at least our initial attention, and may not be devoid even of a measure of attraction. In this very broad sense, the relative eclipse of Jainism and Sāmkhya on the Indian philosophical scene represents the Indian version of the domination of rationalist (here spiritualist) assumptions in the history of Indian philosophy.

The form this new realism, if one may call it that, assumes in modern Western philosophy is somewhat different. This return to empiricism, in the context of a modern philosophy of religion, has led to a renewed emphasis on the *experience* of the reality of God. John Hick has made both these points forcefully. In relation to the world he remarks: "To pursue the same point from a slightly different perspective, if the word 'real' has any meaning for us, we must acknowledge standard or paradigm cases of its correct use. We must be able to point to a clear and unproblematic instance of something's being real. What can this be but some ordinary physical object perceived by the senses? But if table and chairs and houses and people are accepted as paradigm cases of real objects, it becomes self-contradictory to suggest that the whole world of tables and chairs and houses and people may possibly be unreal. By definition, they are not unreal, for they are typical instances of what we mean by real objects".[2]

Nor is he overly permissive in formulating this view, for he is careful to add: "To deny the validity of universal skepticism of the senses is not, however, to deny that there are illusions and hallucinations, or that there are many, and perhaps even inexhaustible, philosophical problems connected with sense perception. It

1. M. Hiriyanna, *Outlines of Indian Philosophy*, p. 172.
2. John H. Hick, *op. cit.*, p. 70.

is one thing to know that a number of sense reports are true and another thing to arrive at their correct philosophical analysis".[1]

While for Jainism the reality of the world must be set alongside the subject who perceives it as real, the argument takes a somewhat different form in modern philosophy of religion. It jumps a step ahead and is used to establish not the subject as real but the experience of the God by the subject also as real as that of the world. As John Hick eloquently puts it: "The biblical writers were (sometimes, though doubtless not at all times) as vividly conscious of being in God's presence as they were of living in a material environment. It is impossible to read their writings with any degree of sensitivity without realizing that to these people God was not a proposition completing a syllogism, or an abstract idea accepted by the mind, but the reality that gave meaning to their lives. Their pages resound and vibrate with the sense of God's presence as a building might resound and vibrate from the tread of some great being walking through it. It would be as sensible for husbands or wives to desire philosophical proof of the existence of their family members (who contribute so much to the meaning of their lives) as for persons of faith to seek proof of the existence of God, within whose purpose they are conscious that they live and move and have their being".

In this way John Hick is able to stake two claims: one, that, "empiricist reasoning is in agreement with the unformulated epistemological assumptions of the Bible. Philosophers of the rationalist tradition, holding that to know means to be able to prove, have been shocked to find that in the Bible, which is the basis of western religion, there is no attempt to demonstrate the existence of God. Instead of professing to establish the reality of God by philosophical reasoning, the Bible takes God's reality for granted";[2] and, two, "that from the point of view of a faith that is biblical in its orientation, the traditional 'theistic proofs' are religiously irrelevant. Even if God could be validly inferred from universally accepted premises, this fact would be of merely aca-

1. *Ibid.*
2. *Ibid.*, p. 70.

demic interest to people who believe that they exist in personal relationship with God and already know God as a living presence".[1]

This latter approach has been called *religious empiricism* and has been formulated in philosophical terms by John Hick as follows: "The issue is not whether it can be established as an item of indubitable public knowledge that God (or the Divine or the Transcendent) exists, or most probably exists, but whether it is rational for those who experience some of life's moments theistically to believe that God exists and to proceed to conduct their lives on that basis".[2]

Rational Belief Without Proofs

At one point, under the influence of rationalism, to believe meant to be able to prove but now the argument has taken a different turn: that it might be fully rational to believe without proof.

We noticed earlier that one definition of faith described it "as the believing of propositions upon insufficient evidence",[3] which resonates with the more general statement of W.K. Clifford that "it is wrong always, everywhere, and for anyone to believe anything upon insufficient evidence".[4] One can see here how pervasive the influence of the rationalist assumption has been.

The issue, as it has developed, turns on what constitutes evidence. John Hick points out that the "idea of evidence normally presupposes a gap between an observed fact, or body of facts, and an *inferred* conclusion. Footprints are evidence everywhere that someone has passed by, but *actually seeing the person pass by is not evidence of this to the observer*, although her report of what she saw may be evidence for someone else".[5]

Several interesting epistemological observations can be made when the statement cited above is viewed in the context of Jaina philosophy. (1) Hindu epistemology distinguishes regularly between perception and inference but the above passage seems to pull them together. This is interesting from a Jaina point of view,

1. *Ibid.*, p. 71.
2. *Ibid.*
3. *Ibid.*, p. 58.
4. *Ibid.* p. 72.
5. *Ibid.*, p. 72, emphases added.

as the single category of *matijñāna*[1] in Jainism, usually translated as ordinary cognition,[2] includes *both* sense perception and deductive reasoning. (2) Jainism distinguishes clearly between (a) seeing the person and (b) a statement vouching for it. This latter form of knowledge constitutes a separate epistemological category called *Śruti-jñāna*. "While matijñāna gives us knowledge by acquaintance, [Śruti-jñāna] gives only knowledge by description".[3] (3) Some Jaina thinkers have made the fine point that "memory, recognition, discursive thought etc. are cases of matijñāna so long as they are not associated with language. They become śruta (scriptural knowledge) as soon as they are associated with words..."[4] (4) The use of the word 'evidence' by Hick touches on a sensitive point in Jaina epistemology.[5] But first a verbal difficulty has to be overcome. A favoured word in Indian epistemology is *pramāna*, usually defined as a means of 'valid knowledge'. Thus, although linguistic usage could complicate the point, to see a person does constitute evidence of the sight of the person, in the sense of *pramāna*. Perhaps one could say that it is 'proof' rather than 'evidence', and this could well be the point Hick wishes to make.

This point leads to what John Hick says next in this context.

> Again, if I hold my hand in front of my eyes, it is appropriate, rational, justifiable to believe that I am seeing my hand. But do I believe this on the basis of *evidence*? Surely not. What would the evidence be? Is it the visual experience of a pinkish-whitish shape, of the kind that we normally call an arm; and do I infer from this that I am seeing my hand? I am not conscious of making any such inference. Even if I did, or if I made it unconsciously, we could then ask—though with increasingly obvious absurdity—on what evidence I believe that I see it. At some point we have to accept that I just have the experience that I have, and that it is rational, appropri-

1. Nathmal Tatia, *op. cit.*, p. 30ff. Also see p. 28.
2. S. Radhakrishnan, *op. cit.*, Vol. I, p. 294. But also see Nathmal Tatia, *op. cit.*, p. 30.
3. *Ibid.*
4. Nathmal Tatia, *op. cit.*, p. 34.
5. *Ibid.*, pp. 56ff.

> ate, and justifiable to be in a belief-state reflecting that experience. Thus, seeing my hand, giving rise to the belief that I am seeing my hand, is an example of rational believing that is appropriately grounded in experience and yet not based upon evidence in an ordinary sense of the word. Nor does it involve any reasoning or argument because there is here no gap between premises and conclusion for reasoning to bridge.[1]

What Hick seems to be saying is that self-evidence does not constitute evidence. Moreover, "our ordinary moment-to-moment perceptual beliefs contradict the principle that *all* rational believing must be based upon adequate evidence. It is not that they are based upon inadequate evidence, but rather that the model of evidence→inference→belief does not apply here. Ordinary perceptual beliefs arise directly out of our experience, and it is entirely appropriate, proper, rational to form these beliefs in this way".[2]

John Hick then extends the range of this line of reasoning to point out that "Perceptual beliefs are by no means the only examples of rationally held beliefs that are not based upon evidence. Other types include believing in self-evident propositions (e.g., 'there is a world'), analytic truths (e.g., '2+2=4'), and uncontroversial reports of your own memory (e.g., 'I had breakfast this morning'), and also the holding of incorrigible beliefs, i.e. beliefs which, when sincerely held, cannot be mistaken, such as 'I am now conscious' or 'I feel pain in my jaw.' *Such beliefs, arising in us directly and not as a result of inference, are often described as basic or foundational.* They are beliefs that are to hold in appropriate circumstances. The idea that our belief-structures are and must be built upon such basic beliefs is called *foundationalism*, although the student should be warned that the term is not always used only in precisely this way".[3]

1. John H. Hick, *op. cit.*, p. 72.
2. *Ibid.*
3. *Ibid.*, p. 72-73, emphasis added.

Rational Foundationalism

John Hick started out by citing W.K. Clifford's statement, doubtless reflecting the rationalist assumption, that "it is wrong always, everywhere, and for anyone to believe anything upon insufficient evidence".[1] Upon further investigation of what constituted evidence, Clifford's statement turned out to be too narrow as a basis for *rational* belief,[2] so that one could "reformulate Clifford's principle', not simply in terms of evidence, but more widely in terms of reasons: We should always have either appropriate experiential grounds or good reasons for our beliefs. Foundationalism adds that such 'good reasons' will ultimately have to appeal to premises that are basic in the sense that they are not derived from further premises".[3]

These basic beliefs fall into two groups: (1) analytical and (2) experiential. Thus two plus two is basic to all, not leaving room for error but beliefs based on perception or memory or religion are, unlike the analytical ones, corrigible. They are not basic in the abstract sense but basic in the concrete sense of being *basic to someone* and hence liable to be in error.[4]

Early in the discussion a parallel was established between religious and perceptual beliefs. Hence it might be useful to probe the basicality of perceptual beliefs more carefully. The room for perceptual error means that one must distinguish between: (1) basic beliefs; and (2) properly basic belief. The second category recognizes the point that while perception involves basicality, the conditions in which it occurs affect the fact whether it is proper or not and if the perception corresponds to object then it is obviously true. Now the question arises: "How...might we establish that a properly basic belief—one that we are rationally justified in holding—is in fact true?"[5]

The problem is this—we have every reason to be confident but there is possibility of error. If I want to check how many fingers

1. *Ibid*, p. 72.
2. *Ibid.*, emphasis added.
3. *Ibid.*, p. 73.
4. *Ibid.*
5. *Ibid.*, p. 74-75.

I have, I count them carefully when unsure of myself. Or, as a post-op procedure, I wiggle my toe to make sure it is there. All this, however, assumes the reliability of sense experience, but we know it is liable to error! Nevertheless, "the appeal from a particular moment of experience to other confirming or disconfirming moments [does help] if we assume that our sense experience is in general veridical, even though also subject to occasional errors. And so the ultimate question then arises: How do we know that the whole realm of sense experience is not delusory—that is consists of nothing but our own subjective states of consciousness? The answer seems to be that we cannot establish this in any noncircular way, but that it is nevertheless rational for us to assume it and to live on the basis of it; and indeed, more strongly, that it would be positively irrational not to. In other words, we have come here to something that is for us truly foundational, something that we just have to accept as a basis both for judgment about the veridical or delusory character of particular perceptions and for our thought and action generally".[1]

Now we are in a position to see how a *foundational* belief may be so called: "We are thus led to distinguish between particular perceptual beliefs (such as the belief that a person sees a tree in front of her) and our general belief in the normally veridical rather than delusory character of sense experience. This latter is equivalent to the assumption that there is a real world of which we are a part and which impinges upon us through our sense organs. Thus if we describe as *basic* such beliefs as 'I see a tree before me' (with its immediate implication that 'There is a tree there'), it would be useful to have a different term for the deeper foundation on which all such beliefs rest, namely our general assumption that through our senses we are interacting with a real physical environment. Let us describe this latter belief as *foundational*".[2]

In the rest of the chapter John Hick tries to apply this analysis to demonstrate the foundational nature of religious belief in theism. In doing so he loses the Jaina. From the Jaina perspective, sensory

1. *Ibid.* p. 74.
2. *Ibid.*

knowledge is *indirect*, not direct. This point is crucial for understanding the Jaina position in this regard. The Jaina position flies in the face of the conventional structure of epistemology of all the other Indian systems, despite their internal differences and even Jaina thinkers could not fully avoid the pressure to conform in this respect.[1]

However, to fully appreciate the Jaina position the original Jaina position must first be resurrected and identified as follows:

> When the problem of pramana (valid knowledge) presented itself before the Jaina thinkers, the term '*jñāna*' (knowledge) was replaced by the word 'pramāna' (valid knowledge). The fundamental basis of the epistemological position of the Jaina logicians can be adequately expressed by the equation *pramāna=samyag-jñāna* (right knowledge). *Mati* (sensuous) and Śruta (scriptural) knowledge were put under *paroksa* (indirect or mediate cognition), and the other three—*avadhi* (visual intuition), *manaparyāya* (intuition of mental modes) and *kevala* (perfect knowledge)—were classified under *pratyaksa* (direct or immediate intuition). This was but natural. The knowledge is *pratyaksa* (direct) or *paroksa* (indirect) according as it is born without or with the help of an external instrument different from the self.[2]

Now the key statement can be made, without causing undue bewilderment, that the "Jain conception of *paroksa* and *pratyaksa* was just the reverse of the traditional Indian conception"[3] and the same applies to traditional Western conceptions. Surprising as it might seem, "knowledge or sentience" is the very essence of the jīva and full religious experience is sought "so that the soul may regain and reveal its true nature of omniscience. Its perception then extends to all objects. Or rather there is no perception at all then, in its ordinary sense, but only a mystic and direct intuition of all things".[4]

1. Nathmal Tatia, *op. cit.*, p. 28-29.
2. *Ibid.*, p. 28.
3. Narendra Nath Bhattacharyya, *Jain Philosophy: Historical Outline* (New Delhi: Munshiram Manoharlal, 1976) p. 160. Also see p. 113-114.
4. M. Hiriyanna, *The Essential of Indian Philosophy*, p. 61.

The question the reader might wish to raise is this. If it may be said of Cartesian argument that "when doubt becomes universal in its scope it becomes meaningless",[1] can the same be said of such knowledge in Jainism?

1. John H. Hick, *op. cit.*, p. 70.

CHAPTER VII

RELIGIOUS LANGUAGE

The Peculiarity of Religious Language

The problem of language in relation to religion focuses on two major issues in the modern philosophy of religion: (1) what special sense "descriptive terms bear when applied to God"[1] and (2) what is "the basic function of religious language".[2] When we say, for instance, that "God is love" then (1) what do we mean by love in this statement? We are using a term born out of human experience to describe a divine attribute. What exactly could it mean?; and (2) What is its purpose? For instance: is the function of this statement to make us more loving rather than provide an accurate description of God?

These problems of religious language, as the examples provided might suggest, are unique to theism. And Jainism, as has been repeatedly noted virtually *ad nauseam* by now, is not theistic in the conventional sense. A little reflection will reveal, however, that religious language does pose a wider problem, not necessarily restricted to theism, inasmuch as when ordinary terms are "applied in religious discourse",[3] they are "used in special ways, differing from their use in ordinary mundane contexts".[4] The word *nirvāna*, for instance, is used in Buddhism in a very special way.[5] This is often the lexical fate of ordinary terms when they are employed in a formal discourse. The word *mass*[6], for instance, has a very

1. John H. Hick, *op. cit.*, p. 82.
2. *Ibid.*
3. *Ibid.*, p. 82.
4. *Ibid.*
5. See R.E.A. Johansson, *The Psychology of Nirvāna* (London: Allen & Unwin, 1969).
6. Philip Babcock Gove, ed., *Webster's Third New International Dictionary* (Springfield, Mass.: G & C. Merriam Company, 1959) p. 1388.

different meaning in physics than it has in ordinary usage. Thus context by itself suffices to initiate a consideration of the way language functions in a religion. The Indian word *dharma*, for instance, has a special meaning in Buddhism[1] as well as Jainism[2], apart from its general connotation.

Not only do secular words acquire special meaning in a context of discourse; it is also worth noting that "in all those cases in which a word occurs both in secular"[3] and in religious or theological context, "its secular meaning is primary, in the sense that it developed first and has accordingly determined the definition of the word".[4]

The Role of Religious Language

The role of religious language consists of describing, or at least pointing to, the reality as propounded in that religion. Western philosophy of religion, therefore, seems preoccupied with the question of God-talk, because God is identified as the ultimate reality in Christianity, or in other monotheistic systems of belief.

What then is the nature of reality according to Jainism, towards describing which it deploys all the linguistic resources at its disposal? In other words, it will be impossible to comprehend the use of religious language within Jainism without an adequate grasp of its fundamental ontology.

The Jaina concept of reality is best arrived at by degrees and by dialectics. One view of reality is represented by some forms of Vedānta in which substance alone is real, and its various changing forms are less so. There is a famous passage, for instance, in the Chāndogya Upanisad (VI.1) which holds that "since in all changes the clay-matter remained permanent, that alone was true, whereas the changes of form and state were but appearances, the nature of which cannot be rationally demonstrated or explained".[5] The

1. Wm. Theodore de Bary, ed., *op. cit.*, Vol. I p. 96 note 4; Ainslie T. Embree, ed. *Sources of Indian Tradition* (second edition) (New York: Columbia University Press, 1988) p. 187 note 19.
2. *Ibid.*, p. 64.
3. John H. Hick, *op. cit.*, p. 83.
4. *Ibid.*
5. Surendranath Dasgupta, *op. cit.*, Vol. I, p. 173-174.

Buddhists take the opposite view, that "what we perceive as clay is some specific quality, what we perceive as jug is also some quality. Apart from these qualities we do not perceive any qualityless substance, which the Upanisad regards as permanent and unchangeable".[1]

So the question remains: is substance alone real, as some Vedāntins argue, or are the modes alone real, as the Buddhists argue?[2] The Jainas looked at the same clay and jug as the Vedāntins and the Buddhists, and came up with the following conclusion: "It is true that qualities of things are changing every minute, but all qualities are not changing. Thus when a jug is made, it means that the clay-lump has been destroyed, a jug has been generated and the clay is permanent, i.e. all production means that some old qualities have been lost, some new ones brought in, and there is some part in it which is permanent. The clay has become lost in some form, has generated itself in another, and remained permanent in still another form. It is by virtue of these unchanged qualities that a thing is said to be permanent though undergoing change".[3]

This simultaneous postulation of permanence, or substance, and change, or mode, instead of rejection of one in favour of the other is a striking characteristic of the Jaina concept of reality. The point illustrated with the help of the examples of the clay and jar may be presented more analytically and less imagistically, as follows:

---

1. *Ibid.*, p. 174.
2. This historical context is not without its own interest. "The Jains we know were the contemporaries of Buddha and possibly of some of the Upanisads too, and they had also a solution to offer. They held that it was not true that substance alone was true and qualities were mere false and illusory appearances. Further, it was not true as the Buddhists said, that there was no permanent substance but merely the change of passing qualities, for both these represent two extreme views and are contrary to experience. Both of them, however, contain some elements of truth but not the whole truth as given in experience" (*Ibid.*). Jainism may be viewed in an Upanisadic context in yet another way. "The Upanisadic conception of reality, according to our explanation, is of two kinds – one which takes change as actual and the other as unreal. Of these, the Jaina view resembles the former; only it regards reality as multiple in its character. It is what changes almost perpetually or is dynamic, and yet keeps its identity throughout" (M. Hiriyanna, *The Essentials of Indian Philosophy*, p. 65)
3. Surendranath Dasgupta, *op. cit.*, Vol. I, p. 174, 175.

> Experience shows that in all changes there are three elements: (1) that some collocations of qualities appear to remain unchanged; (2) that some new qualities are generated; (3) that some old qualities are destroyed... Thus when a lump of gold is turned into a rod or a ring, all the specific qualities which come under the connotation of the word "gold" are seen to continue, though the forms are successively changed, and with each such change some of its qualities are lost and some new ones are acquired. Such being the case, the truth comes to this, that there is always a permanent entity as represented by the permanence of such qualities as lead us to call it a substance in spite of all its diverse changes. The nature of being (*sat*) then is neither the absolutely unchangeable, nor the momentary changing qualities or existences, but involves them both.[1]

The Jaina word for substance is *dravya* and for mode *paryāya* (along with which the word *guṇa* or quality is also used).[2]

The Problem of Religious Language

This conception of reality may be described as that of relative pluralism[3] or pluralistic realism.[4] It poses a special problem for religious language all its own, given its dynamic, relative and plural

1. *Ibid.*, p. 174, 175.
2. See B.K. Matilal, *op. cit.*, p. 35. "We shall now understand the exact significance of the definition of reality given in the system, that it is characterized by origination and destruction, as well as by permanence. The origination and destruction relate to the modes (*paryāya*) of reality; and permanence, to their substratum. It is reality, in this sense, that is divided into *jīva* and *ajīva* with its fivefold variety as mentioned above. All these six kinds of reality are termed substances (dravya)—a term which connotes that it has qualities (*guna*) and modes (*paryāya*). The distinction between qualities and modes, however, is not very clear; and the recognition of the former is probably due, as has been suggested, to the influence of other doctrines. Of these six substances, all but time, besides being real, are extended (*asti-kāya*). Time is real, but has no spatial extension. It is an entity of only one dimension". (H. Hiriyanna, *The Essentials of Indian Philosophy*, p. 66-67)
3. Surendranath Dasgupta, *op. cit.*, Vol. I, p. 175.
4. S. Radhakrishnan, *op. cit.*, Vol. I, Chapter VI.

character. As Surendranath Dasgupta explains: "This conception of being as the union of the permanent and change brings us naturally to the doctrine of Anekāntavāda or what we may call relative pluralism as against the extreme absolutism of the Upanisads and the pluralism of the Buddhists. The Jains regarded all things as *anekānta* (*na-ekānta*), or in other words they held that nothing could be affirmed absolutely, as all affirmations were true only under certain conditions and limitations."[1]

The reader is likely to miss the complexity involved here unless it is specified. The examples of a jug (of clay) and gold were used in the preceding discussion. Let us now combine the two into a gold-jug for illustrative purposes. The complexities one runs into may then be described as follows: "Thus speaking of a gold jug, we see that its existence as a substance (*dravya*) is of the nature of a collocation of atoms and not as any other substance such as space (*ākāśa*), i.e. a gold jug is a *dravya* only in one sense of the term and not in every sense; so it is a *dravya* in the sense that it is a collocation of atoms and not a *dravya* in the sense of space or time (*kāla*). It is thus both a *dravya* and not a dravya at one and the same time".[2] The point stretches further: "*Again* it is atomic in the sense that it is a composite of earth-atoms and not atomic in the sense that it is not a composite of water-atoms. *Again* it is a composite of earth-atoms only in the sense that gold is a metallic modification of earth, and not any other modification of earth as clay or stone. Its being constituted of metal-atoms is *Again* true in the sense that it is made up of gold-atoms in the sense of melted and unsullied gold and not as gold in the natural condition. It is *Again* made up of such unsullied and melted gold as has been hammered and shaped by the goldsmith Devadatta and not by Yajñadatta".[3] The point has not unravelled itself yet. "Its being made up of atoms conditioned as above is *Again* only true in the sense that the collocation has been shaped as a jug and not as a pot and so on. Thus proceeding in a similar manner the Jains say that all affirmations are true of a thing only in a certain limited sense".[4] And so on.

1. Surendranath Dasgupta, *op. cit.*, Vol. I, p. 175.
2. *Ibid.*, p. 175.
3. *Ibid.*, p. 176, emphasis added.
4. *Ibid.*, emphasis added.

Thus the basic point to contend with is that "*All things* (*vastu*) *thus possess an infinite number of qualities (anantadharmātmakam vastu), each of which can only be affirmed in a particular sense.* Such an ordinary thing as a jug will be found to be the object of an infinite number of affirmations and the possessor of an infinite number of qualities from infinite points of view, which are all true in certain restricted senses and not absolutely".[1] The situation is further complicated by the fact that the assertions can be positive as well as negative. This opens another can. "Thus in the positive relation riches cannot be affirmed of poverty but in the negative relation such an affirmation is possible as when we say 'the poor man has no riches.' The poor man possesses riches not in a positive but in a negative way. Thus in some relation or other anything may be affirmed of any other thing, and again in other relations the very same thing cannot be affirmed of it. *The different standpoint from which things (though possessed of infinite determinations) can be spoken of as possessing this or that quality or as appearing in relation to this or that, are technically called naya*".[2]

Life is made somewhat easier by the fact that although in principle "nayas...are but points of view, or aspects of looking at things, and such infinite in number",[3] a broad classification of them into seven categories is available. If one starts out with the twofold division of *dravyanaya* or substance standpoint, and paryāyanaya or mode standpoint, the following summary might be helpful here, which explains the Jaina doctrine known as:

> *nayavāda*, the theory of standpoint, or ways of approaching an object of observation or study. The first three of these are connected with the object itself (*dravyārthika*), and the latter four with its modifications and the words used to describe it (*paryāyārthika*). (1) A mango tree maybe considered simultaneously as an individual having a definite size and shape and as a member of the species "mango tree"; (2) it may be treated merely as a representative of the "universal" mango tree, and as corresponding to the general concept of a mango

1. *Ibid.*, emphasis added.
2. *Ibid.*, emphasis added.
3. *Ibid.*, p. 178.

tree, without taking its individual qualities into account; or (3) it may be considered merely as an individual, without taking note of its specific qualities. Further it may be thought of (4) as it is at the present moment, for instance as bearing ripe fruit, without any regard to its past as a sapling or its future as firewood. (5) We may think of it from the point of view of its name "mango", considering all the synonyms of that name, and their implications. These synonyms may be subtly differentiated, and (6) we may consider their nuances and connotations. Finally (7) we may consider an object in its relation to a given epithet; thus by referring to a hero as a "lion" we mentally abstract all his unlionlike qualities, and think of him only as a being of strength and courage.[1]

Ontology, Epistemology and Language

The seven standpoints have often been grouped into two sets. According to one such scheme "the first four standpoint (1 through 4) are classified as the standpoint of things while the last three (5 through 7) are classified as the standpoint of the word". B.K. Matilal remarks: "using modern terminology, one may say that the first four are concerned with *ontological* distinctions while the last three with semantic distinctions".[2] A.L. Basham refers to these at one place as *epistemological*[3] (by implication) rather than ontological but then immediately speaks of Jaina systems of "ontological and epistemological relativity".[4]

The point I am trying to make is that the ontological, the epistemological and the linguistic dimensions are closely intertwined in Jainism, specially if one recognizes that "each of these seven nayas has a larger extent than the one which follows. Naigama [the first] has the largest extent and evambhūta [the last] the least".[5] Then one realizes that the scheme is aiming at precision

1. A.L. Basham, *The Wonder That Was India* (London: Sidgwick & Jackson, 1988 [third revised edition]) p. 502-503.
2. B.K. Matilal, *op. cit.*, p. 42, emphasis added.
3. A.L. Basham, *The Wonder That Was India*, p. 503.
4. *Ibid.*
5. S. Radhakrishnan, *op. cit.*, p. 301.

as it converges on semantics, and that these three need to be looked at in their own right, since many issues in Indian philosophy turn on grammar.[1]

Reality and Conditionality

The Jainas refine the religious use of language even further by pointing out that these varied standpoint are not only different, but also conditional. If "anyone regards the interpretation of his point of view as being absolutely true to the exclusion of all other points of view", then "this is their error (*nayābhasa*), for each standpoint represents only one of the many points of view from which a thing may be looked at".[2] To avoid this pitfall the conditionality of the affirmation must be recognized:

> Affirmations or judgments according to any naya or standpoint cannot therefore be absolute, for even contrary affirmations of the very selfsame things may be held to be true from other points of view. The truth of each affirmation is thus only conditional, and inconceivable from the absolute point of view. To guarantee correctness therefore each affirmation should be preceded by the phrase syāt (may be). This will indicate that the affirmation is only relative, made somehow, from some point of view and under some reservations and not in any sense absolute. There is no judgment which

1. Arvind Sharma, *A Hindu Perspective on the Philosophy of Religion* (London: Macmillan, 1990) p. 87-88, 89 note 23. For a detailed explication of the Jaina doctrine adumbrated here see B.K. Matilal, *op. cit.*, p. 45; etc.
2. Surendranath Dasgupta, *op. cit.*, Vol. I, p. 178. The preceding remarks are also worth citing: "The four *nayas* alluded to are *nigama, saṅgraha, vyavahāra* and jusūtra. The *nayas* as we have already said are but points of view, or aspects of looking at things, and as such are infinite in number. The above four represent only a broad classification of these. The Jains hold that the *Nyāya-vaiśeśika*, the Vedānta, the *Sānkhya*, and the Buddhist, have each tried to interpret and systematize experience from one of the above four points of view, and each regards the interpretation from his point of view as being absolutely true to the exclusion of all other points of view. This is their error (*nayābhāsa*), for each standpoint represents only one of the many points of view from which a thing can be looked at. The affirmations from any point of view are thus true in a limited sense and under limited conditions infinite numbers of affirmations may be made of things from infinite points of view".

is absolutely true, and no judgment which is absolutely false. All judgments are true in some sense and false in another. This brings us to the famous Jaina doctrine of Syādvāda.[1]

Syādvāda as a doctrine is itself capable of further elaboration.[2]

---

1. *Ibid.*
2. *Ibid.*, p. 179-180: "The doctrine of *Syādvāda* holds that since the most contrary characteristics of infinite variety may be associated with a thing, affirmation made from whatever standpoint (*naya*) cannot be regarded as absolute. All affirmations are true (in some *syādasti* or "may be it is" sense); all affirmations are false in some sense; all affirmations are indefinite or inconceivable in some sense (*syādavaktavya*); all affirmations are true as well as false in some sense (*syādasti syānnāsti*); all affirmations are true as well as indefinite (*syādasti cāvaktavyaśca*); all affirmations are false as well as indefinite; all affirmations are true and false and indefinite in some sense (*syādasti syānnāsti syādavaktavyaśca*). Thus we may say "the jug is" or the jug has being, but it is more correct to say explicitly that "may be (syāt) that the jug is," otherwise if "being here is taken absolutely of any and every kind of being, it might also mean that there is a lump of clay or a pillar, or a cloth or any other thing. The existence here is limited and defined by the form of the jug. "The jug is" does not mean absolute existence but a limited kind of existence as determined by the form of the jug, "The jug is" thus means that a limited kind of existence, namely the jug-existence is affirmed and not existence in general in the absolute or unlimited sense, for then the sentence "the jug is" might as well mean "the clay is," "the tree is," "the cloth is," etc. Again the existence of the jug is determined by the negation of all other things in the world; each quality or characteristic (such red colour) of the jug is apprehended and defined by the negation of all the infinite varieties (such as black, blue, golden), etc., of its class, and it is by the combined negation of all the infinite number of characteristics or qualities other than those constituting the jug that a jug may be apprehended or defined. What we call the being of the jug is thus the non-being of all the rest except itself. Thus though looked at from one point of view the judgment " the jug is" may mean affirmation of being, looked at from another point of view it means an affirmation of non-being (of all other objects). Thus of the judgment "the jug is" one may say, may be it is an affirmation of being (*syādasti*), may be it is a negation of being (*syānnāsti*); or I may proceed in quite another way and say that "the jug is" means "this jug is here," which naturally indicates that "this jug is not there" and thus the judgment "the jug is" (i.e. is here) also means that "the jug is not there," and so we see that the affirmation of the being of the jug is true only of this place and false of another, and this justifies us in saying that "may be that in some sense the jug is," and "may be in some sense that the jug is not." Combining these two aspects we may say that in some sense "may be that the jug is," and in some sense "may be

Problem of Language Revisited

The problem of language in the modern philosophy of religion basically turns on the issue of how are descriptions of religious reality are to be understood and whether religious language functions cognitively or noncognitively. In the Jaina context the issue is very different, and, in a sense, it fuses the two issues of modern philosophy of religion. The function of religious language is cognitive but the reality to be described in Jainism is so complex that it stretches linguisticality to its maximum. In this, it mimics the problem of understanding descriptions of God. I say 'mimics' because in theistic situations the problem of description is caused by the transcendent quality of the referent in relation to the world and in the Jaina case by the nature of the reality of the world itself.

This complexity is such that according to one understanding of *syādvāda*, one is led via the conditionality of predications to the reality itself. For if the initial issue raised was not: *is a thing permanent or is it impermanent*, but rather *is there a thing* at all, whether permanent or impermanent, then it would shift the gear from the ontological to the ontic and compel us to rearrange our priorities. At this stage in the discussion, however, the matter is best let to rest as a suggestion.[1]

---

that the jug is not." We understood here that if we put emphasis on the side of the characteristics constituting being, we may say "the jug is, " but if we put emphasis on the other side, we may say "the jug is not." Both the affirmations hold good of the jug according as the emphasis is put on the other side. But if without emphasis on either side we try to comprehend the two opposite and contradictory judgments regarding the jug, we see that the nature of the jug or of the existence of the jug is indefinite, unspeakable and inconceivable – *avaktavya*, for how can we affirm both being and non-being of the same thing, and yet such is the nature of things that we cannot but do it. Thus all affirmations are true, are not true, are both true and untrue, and are thus unspeakable, inconceivable, and indefinite. Combining these four again we derive another three, (1) that in some sense it may be that the jug is, and (2) is yet unspeakable, or (3) that the jug is not and is unspeakable, or finally that the jug is, in not, and is unspeakable. Thus Jains hold that no affirmation, or judgment, is absolute in its nature, each is true in its own limited sense only, and for each one of them any of the above seven alternatives (technically called saptabhagī) holds good."

1. See M. Hiriyanna, *The Essentials of Indian Philosophy*, p. 67-68: "Broadly speaking there were three separate ways in which reality was conceived at the time when this theory was formulated. Some said, "*It always is*" (asti); others, "It never is" (nāsti); and still others thought that reality was inscrutable, and that it did not therefore admit of being expressed in either of these two ways

Be that as it may, we must not lose sight of the basic Jaina insight in terms of religious language in the midst of its various elaborations; "that the world is more complex than it seems, that reality is much more subtle than we are inclined to believe, and that our knowledge is less certain than we think".[1]

(*avaktya*). Jainism holds that none of these views is wholly correct. Each refers to but a single aspect of reality and is right only if we take it in relation to that aspect and not absolutely, as its supporters contend. It is this *relative character* of out knowledge of reality that is made known through the *saptabhangī*; and it consists of seven steps since there are seven, and only seven, ways of combining the three predicates, taking them singly, in twos and all together.

To state the first four steps of the scheme: (1) maybe, a thing is; (2) maybe, it is not; (3) maybe, it is and is not; (4) maybe, it is inexpressible. In the case of a golden ornament, for example, we may say that (1) it exists, i.e. as gold, but that (2) it does not exist, i.e. as silver (say). As a consequence of this double predication, we may go farther and postulate that (3) it both is and is not. From what has been stated thus far, it is clear that when we say the ornament is, we do not mean that it only is as something, but also that it is not as something else. The latter idea, however, is implicit, and not explicit like the former. The reverse holds true when we say that it is not. The third step is merely a combination of these two statements; and the emphasis is to be understood as being laid on the two elements in the predicate *successively*. Now it may be asked whether these two elements can be predicated of the ornament *simultaneously*, laying equal emphasis on both. The answer to this question, one expects, would be in the negative; but the Jains, with their comprehensive view of reality, refuse to regard any predicate as inadmissible in respect of it, and give an affirmative reply. They, however, add that the predicate cannot then be expressed by any word in the language, the implied significance being that reality is from one standpoint, inscrutable. These statements should not be taken to clash with what are known in logic as the laws of identity and contradiction, for those laws apply only to reality conceived as simple and static, and not as extremely complex and infinitely variable as here. The remaining three steps of the scheme are: (5) maybe, a thing is and is inexpressible; (6) maybe, a thing is not and is inexpressible; (7) maybe, a thing is, is not and is inexpressible. They are derived by combining the fourth step successively with the first three, all of which refer to the expressible aspects of reality. This relativistic view has become so essential a part of Jainsm that it is often designated as the "doctrine of maybe" (*syādvāda*) or the doctrine of standpoints".

1. See Wm. Theodore de Bary, ed., *op. cit.*, Vol. I, p. 75. A. L. Basham notes elsewhere" "Modern logicians might make short work of these rather pedantic systems of ontological and epistemological relativity, but they have a fundamental quality of breadth and realism, implying a full realization that the world is more complex and subtle than we think it, and that what is true of a thing in one of its aspects may at the same time be false in another" (*The Wonder That Was India*, p. 503).

CHAPTER VIII

RELIGIOUS LANGUAGE AND TRUTH

Introduction

In Western philosophy of religion, on account of its theistic presuppositions, the question of verifiability assumes a special significance for three reasons: (1) Christian and Jewish faiths make *theological* statements; (2) they accord to them the status of *factual* statements; (3) these then have to be examined from the point of view of analytical philosophy, which deals with factual, but *actual* and not theological statements. Given this background it is clear why "the development within twentieth century philosophy of a criterion by which to distinguish the factual from the nonfactual is directly relevant to the study of religious language".[1]

As Jainism is nontheistic, the first of the above three points ceases to be relevant. However, as Jainism deals with the reality of the world on its own ground as solidly as Logical Positivism, it provides an excellent foil for examining the Logical Positivist position. Moreover, as it is nevertheless still a religion, although not a theistic one, such a discussion cannot but be relevant for the study of religious language.

The Question of Verifiability

Prior to the rise of the movement known as Logical Positivism, the veracity of a proposition could be determined by a "direct examination as to its truth or falsity".[2] Jainism accepts this general formulation. It does not hold, as some other schools of Indian thought are willing to maintain, that the validity of all knowledge

1. John H. Hick, *op. cit.*, p. 100.
2. *Ibid.*

is proved by knowledge itself. According to Jainism, "both logically and psychologically the validity of knowledge depends upon outward correspondence (*saṁvāda*) with facts".[1]

Logical Positivism introduced another element in this situation, by adding another stipulation—that the proposition must be meaningful. The word "meaningful" here must be understood logically rather than psychologically. That is to say, to claim a proposition is meaningful, that it has meaning means that

> it has factual or cognitive meaning, it is to say that it is in principle verifiable, or at least "probabilifiable," by reference to human experience. This means, in effect, that its truth or falsity must make some possible experienceable difference. If its truth or falsity makes no difference that could possibly be observed, the proposition is cognitively meaningless; it does not embody a factual assertion.[2]

John Hick offers an interesting example to illustrate the force of the new position.

> Suppose, for example, the startling news is announced one morning that overnight the entire physical universe has instantaneously doubled in size and that the speed of light has doubled. At first, this news seems to point to a momentous scientific discovery. All the items composing the universe, including our own bodies, are now twice as big as they were yesterday. But questions concerning the evidence for this report must be raised. How can anyone know that the universe has doubled in size? What observable difference does it make whether this is so or not; what events or appearances are supposed to reveal it? On further reflection, it becomes clear that there *could not* be any evidence for this particular proposition, for if the entire universe has doubled and the speed of light has doubled with it, our measurements have also doubled and we can never know that any change

1. Surendranath Dasgupta, *op. cit.*, Vol. I, p. 188.
2. John H. Hick, *op. cit.*, p. 101.

> has taken place. If our measuring rod has expanded with the objects to be measured, it cannot measure their expansion. In order adequately to acknowledge the systematic impossibility of testing such a proposition, it seems best to classify it as (cognitively) meaningless. It first seemed to be a genuinely factual assertion, but under scrutiny it proves to lack the basic characteristic of an assertion, namely, that it must make an experienceable difference whether the facts are as alleged or not.[1]

A similar question was posed to Mahāvīra by Skandhaka and the manner in which Mahāvīra answers it provides an interesting clue to the Jaina approach to the meaningfulness of a proposition.

> There has been the following question in your mind, Skandhaka, which you have thought about, considered, deliberated and posed to ask: 'Is the world finite (with an end), or is it infinite?' This can be explained as follows: I have given instruction about the world, Skandhaka, in four ways: They are: following the point of view of the substance, that of area-measurement, that of time, and that of modifications.
>
> Now, from the point of view of substance, the world is one, and therefore, finite (i.e. countable in number). From the point of view of its area-measurement, the world is, again finite (i.e. its numerical calculation is possible), for its length and breadth are each measured as asaṁkhyāta $10{,}000{,}000^2$ *yojanas.* (This is following the Jaina mythological account of the universe found in *Karmagrantha.*) And its circumference is measured again, as asaṁkhyāta $10{,}000{,}000^2$ *yojanas.* (The latter asaṁkhyāta number must be a greater number than the former.)
>
> From the point of view of time, the world does not have an end (i.e. infinite), for it did not cease to exist at any time, neither does it cease to exist (now), nor will it cease to exist at any time, it was, it is and it will be; it is constant, eternal, permanent, imperishable, indestructible, and always existent.

---

1. *Ibid.*

> From the point of view of modifications, the world is infinite (i.e. uncountable in number), for it has limitless modifications of colour, smell, taste and touch, it has limitless modification in the form of configuration, it has limitless forms of being heavy and light, and limitless states of formless modifications (*a-guru-laghu-paryāya*).
>
> Therefore, Skandhaka, the world is finite from the point of view of its substance, finite (i.e. measurable) from the point of view of its area, (but) infinite from the point of view of time (duration) and also infinite (uncountable) from the point of view of its modifications.[1]

It is clear, then, that for a proposition to be meaningful it must be brought in meaningful relation to *dravya* (substance), *kstra* (area-measurement), *kāla* (time) and *rūpa* (modification).

If we now apply this analysis to John Hick's example, we find that his example involved substance (universe), area-measurement (doubled); time (doubled) and form (doubled). The following remarks of S. Radhakrishnan, made in another context in his discussion of Jainism, are extremely helpful here.

> A thing is what it is and is not what it is not. According to this view, all negation has a positive basis. Even imaginary concepts like skyflower possess a positive basis in the two reals sky and flower, though their combination is unreal. *It emphasises the fundamental truth that distinction is necessary for thought.* A thing which has nothing from which it can be distinguished is unthinkable. The absolute devoid of distinctions within as well as without is truly unthinkable. For all things which are objects of thought *are* in one sense and *are not* in another.[2]

What Hick called "experienceable difference" may be brought in relation to "distinction" in the above passage. Jainism would seem to concur on this point with Hick.

Bimal K. Matilal also draws certain conclusions from the passage cited earlier. First of all, he draws attention to the fact that by

1. Cited in Bimal Krishna Matilal, *op. cit.*, p. 20-21.
2. S. Radhakrishnan, *op. cit.*, Vol. I, p. 304, emphasis added.

applying (linguistic) analysis to the "unexplained" questions the various possible senses are uncovered: "It is clear from the above that when Mahāvīra tried to answer the so-called *avyākata* questions through the *vibhajya* method, he had analysed the different senses of, and thereby clarified the ambiguity contained in, such predicate-expressions, 'infinite' and 'finite.' 'Infinite' may mean 'limitless in number or measurement' or 'everlasting.' Similarly, 'finite' may mean 'limited in number or measurement' or 'of limited duration.'"[1] Then he notes the further fact that not only are various senses of the statement taken into account, all the possible senses are accounted for.

> Notice that all these senses have been taken into account in Mahāvīra's method of analysis. One can thus agree with the principle of Mahāvīra without necessarily agreeing with the Jaina mythical account of the universe and man.[2]

Finally, B.K. Matilal distinguishes Mahāvīra's approach from that of the Buddha.

> Notice also that Mahāvīra's analysis differed from that of the Buddha in that the Buddha maintained his doctrine of the Middle Way by rejecting the two alternative questions, positive and negative, while Mahāvīra came closer to the anenkānta-vāda by accepting both alternatives with proper qualifications and conditionalization.[3]

We revert now to John Hick's discussion of the verifiability criterion. He points out that

> The basic principle-representing a modified version of the original verifiability principle of logical positivists—that a factual assertion is one whose truth or falsity makes some experienceable difference, has been applied to theological propositions.[4]

As an application of this principle one may cite, with him, this famous parable.

1. B.K. Matilal, *op. cit.*, p. 22.
2. *Ibid.*
3. *Ibid.*
4. John H. Hick, *op. cit.*, p. 101.

Two people return to their long-neglected garden and find among the weeds a few of the old plants surprisingly vigorous. One says to the other " it must be that a gardener has been coming and doing something about these plants." Upon inquiry they find that no neighbor has ever seen anyone at work in their garden. The first man says to the other "He must have worked while people slept." The other says, "No, someone would have heard him and besides anybody who cared about the plants would have kept down these weeds." The first man says, "Look at the way these are arranged. There is purpose and a feeling for beauty here. I believe that someone comes, someone invisible to mortal eyes. I believe that the more carefully we look the more we will find confirmation of this." They examine the garden ever so carefully and sometimes they come on new things suggesting that a gardener comes and sometimes they come on new things suggesting the contrary and even that a malicious person has been at work. Besides examining the garden carefully they also study what happens to gardens left without attention. Each learns all the other learns about this and about the garden. Consequently, when after all this, one says "I still believe a gardener comes" while the other says "I don't" their different words now reflect no difference as to what they have found in the garden, no difference as to what they would find in the garden if they looked further and no difference about how fast untended gardens fall into disorder. At this stage, in this context, the gardener hypothesis has ceased to be experimental, the difference between one who accepts and one who rejects it is not now a matter of the one expecting something the other does not expect. What is the difference between them? The one says, "A gardener comes unseen and unheard. He is manifested only in his works with which we are all familiar," the other says "There is no gardener" and with this difference in what they say about the gardener goes a difference in how they feel towards the garden, in spite of the fact that neither expects anything of it which the other does not expect.[1]

1. Cited in *Ibid.*, p. 101-102.

John Hick concludes after examining the various options that in this case "neither of the rival positions is, even in principle, verifiable".[1]

What would be a Jaina take on this? It seems to me reasonable to propose, that, from a Jaina point of view, the proposition is *predicable but not verifiable.* It is not verifiable for the obvious reasons but it is predicable as *avaktavya* or inexpressible. It is inexpressible *not* because "it does not...admit of being expressed in either or the two ways",[2] namely, that the gardener "comes" and "cometh not" but because it must be taken to be a unitary whole, a primary predicate".[3] The *philosophical theist* could say that 'from *a certain point of view* it is' (the gardener comes; God is) and is inexpressible and the philosophical atheist could say that "from *a certain point of view* it is not" (the gardner does not come; there is no God). In other words, the meta-assumption, according to Jainism, may be capable of inclusion in the proposition.

But perhaps more can be said. In order to prepare the ground for it, let us begin by sharing John Hick's remarks on the parable, famously proposed by Wisdom.

> Wisdom is here suggesting that the theist and the atheist do not disagree about the empirical (experienceable) facts, or about any observations which they anticipate in the future; they are, instead, reacting in different ways to the same set of facts. Understanding them in this way, we can no longer say in any usual sense that one is right and the other wrong. They both really feel about the world in the ways that their words indicate. However, expressions of feelings do not constitute assertions about the world. We would have to speak, instead, of these different feelings being more or less satisfying or valuable: as Santaya said, religions are not true or false but better or worse. According to Wisdom there is no disagreement about the experienceable facts, the settlement of which would oetermine whether the theist or the atheist

1. *Ibid.*, p. 102.
2. M. Hiriyanna, *The Essentials of Indian Philosophy*, p. 67.
3. B.K. Matilal, *op. cit.*, p. 56.

> is right. In other words, neither of the rival positions is, even in principle, verifiable.[1]

At issue is the factual assertion of the existence of God and its verifiability. Jainism admits five kinds of knowledge (1) *mati* (ordinary cognition); (2) *śruti* (testimony); (3) *avadhi* (clairvoyance); (4) *manahparyāya* (telepathy) and (5) *kevala* (prefect knowledge). Two points need to be noted here: that (1) the doctrine of *naya*, although apparently applicable to *mati*, is developed specially in case of *śruti*, "Since different interpretations of the scriptural texts come up for discussion"[2] and that (2) "the first three kinds of knowledge are liable to be in error, *while the last two cannot be wrong*".[3]

Thus if the *tīrthankara*, who is in possession of *kevala jñāna*, has declared non-existence of God, then, from the point of view of the Jaina, we can *also say that from a certain point of view it is not and is inexpressible.*

The Question of Falsifiability

Something may not be verifiable but it may be falsifiable. Thus the next logical move, in theistic discourse, is to focus on a slightly different version of the question: is the existence of God falsifiable? Hence "the debate next shifted from the idea of verifiability to the complementary idea of falisifiability. The question was posed whether there is any conceivable event which, if it were to occur, would decisively refute theism? Are there any possible developments of our experience with which theism would be incompatible, or is it equally compatible with whatever may happen? Is anything ruled out by belief in God?"[4]

The issue was taken up memorably by Anthony Flew, who responded as follows:

> Now it often seems to people who are not religious as if there was no conceivable event or series of events the occur-

1. John H. Hick, *op. cit.*, p. 102.
2. S. Radhakrishnan, *op. cit.*, Vol. I, p. 295.
3. *Ibid.*
4. John H. Hick, *op. cit.*, p. 102.

> rence of which would be admitted by sophisticated religious people to be a sufficient reason for conceding "There wasn't a God after all" or "God does not really love us then." Someone tells us that God loves us as a father loves his children. We are reassured. But then we see a child dying of inoperable cancer of the throat. His earthly father is driven frantic in his efforts to help, but his Heavenly Father reveals no obvious sign of concern. Some qualification is made–God's love is "not a merely human love" or it is "an inscrutable love," perhaps—and we realize that such sufferings are quite compatible with the truth of the assertion that "God loves us as a father (but, of course...)" We are reassured again. But then perhaps we ask: what is this assurance of God's (appropriately qualified) love worth, what is this apparent guarantee really a guarantee against? Just what would have to happen not merely (morally and wrongly) to tempt but also (logically and rightly) to entitle us to say "God does not love us" or even "God does not exist"? I therefore put...the simple central questions, "What would have to occur or to have occurred to constitute for you a disproof of the love of, or of the existence of, God?"[1]

According to Flew, then, the existence of God is not falsifiable. What does a Jaina philosopher have to say to this? Just this, that "when a proposition is unconditionally asserted it becomes falsifiable".[2] In other words, from a Jaina point of view, the way

1. Cited, *Ibid.*, p. 102-103.
2. B.K. Matilal, *op. cit.*, p. 2-3. The entire passage bears citing: "When a proposition is unconditionally asserted, it becomes *falsifiable.* An unconditionally asserted metaphysical proposition, such as "*x* is *f*" ascribes the property "f-ness" to the subject. And it can be falsified when its contradictory "*x* is not *f*" is shown to be true. Thus, a metaphysical thesis of a particular school is usually rejected by a rival school which puts forward a (directly or indirectly) contradictory thesis. Jainism says that the lesson to be drawn from such age-old philosophic disputes is the following: Each school asserts its thesis and claims it to be the absolute truth, and thus it does not really wish to understand the point that is being made by the opposite side. The rival schools, by their arguments and counter arguments, only encourage dogmatism and intoleration in philosophy. This, according to the Jainas, is the evil of ekānta 'one-sided' philosophies. But the philosophic propositions of rival schools

the issue of God's falsifiability has been set up puts the cart before the horse. As Flew's statement demonstrates, because the proposition as been set up unconditionally, it is not so much *unfalsifiable as continually falsifiable.*

Eschatological Verification

Given the preceding situation, in which theistic discourse found itself pushed philosophically against the wall of logical positivism, John Hick came up with the idea of eschatological verification. The concept comprises the following five points:

> 1. The verification of a factual assertion is not the same as a logical demonstration of it. The central core of the idea of verification is the removal of grounds for rational doubt. That a proposition, *p*, is verified means that something happens that makes it clear that *p* is true. A question is settled, so that there is no longer room for reasonable doubt concerning it. The way in which such grounds are excluded varies, of course, with the subject matter, but the common feature in all cases of verification is the ascertaining of truth by the removal of grounds for rational doubt. Whenever such grounds have been removed, we rightly speak of verification having taken place.
>
> 2. Sometimes it is necessary to put oneself in a certain position or to perform some particular operation as a prerequisite of verification, For example, one can only verify "There is a table in the next room" by going into the next room; however, it is to be noted that one is not compelled to do this.
>
> 3. Therefore, although "verifiable" normally means "publicly verifiable" (i.e., capable in principle of being verified by anyone), it does not follow that a given verifiable proposition

could be integrated together under the *Anekānta* system. In other words, these rival propositions can be said to capture the truth when and only when they are asserted with proper qualifications or conditions. This is what the *anekānta* doctrine teaches. How can one *conditionalize one's philosophic proposition*? Add a "syāt" particle to the proposition and you have captured the truth!"

has in fact been or will in fact ever be verified by everyone. The number of people who verify a particular true proposition depends upon all manner of contingent factors.

4. It is possible for a proposition to be in principle verifiable if true but not in principle falsifiable if false. Consider, for example, the proposition that "there are three successive sevens in the decimal determination of *p*." So far as the value of *p* has been worked out, it does not contain a series of three sevens; but since the operation can proceed *ad infinitum* it will always be true that a triple seven may occur at a point not yet reached in anyone's calculations. Accordingly, the proposition may one day be verified if it is true but can never be falsified if it is false.

5. The hypothesis of continued conscious existence after bodily death provides another instance of a proposition that is verifiable if true but not falsifiable if false. This hypothesis entails a prediction that one will, after the date of one's bodily death, have conscious experiences, including the experience of remembering that death. This is a prediction that will be verified in one's own experience if it is true but that cannot be falsified if it is false. That is to say, it can be false, but *that* it is false can never be a fact of which anyone has experiential knowledge. This principle does not undermine the meaningfulness of the survival hypothesis, for if its prediction is true, it will be known to be true.[1]

It is clear that all these propositions are necessary because Christian theism possesses only a post-mortem eschatology. This becomes all the more clear when we take the following parable of John Hick into account:

> Two people are travelling together along a road. One of them believes that it leads to the Celestial City, the other that it leads nowhere; but since this is the only road there is, both must travel it. Neither has been this way before; therefore,

1. John H. Hick, *op. cit.*, p. 103-104.

> neither is able to say what they will find around each corner. During their journey they meet with moments of refreshment and delight, and with moments of hardship and danger. All the time one of them thinks of the journey as a pilgrimage to the Celestial City. She interprets the pleasant parts as encouragements and the obstacles as trials of her purpose and lessons in endurance, prepared by the sovereign of that city and designed to make of her a worthy citizen of the place when at last she arrives. The other, however, believes none of this, and sees their journey as an unavoidable and aimless ramble. Since he has no choice in the matter, he enjoys the good and endures the bad. For him there is no Celestial City to be reached, no all-encompassing purpose ordaining their journey; there is only the road itself and the luck of the road in good weather and in bad.
>
> During the course of the journey, the issue between them is not an experimental one. That is to say, they do not entertain different expectations about the coming details of the road, but only about its ultimate destination. Yet when they turn the last corner, it will be apparent that one of them has been right all the time and the other wrong. Thus, although the issue between them has not been experimental, it has nevertheless been a real issue. They have not merely felt differently about the road, for one was feeling appropriately and the other inappropriately in relation to the actual state of affairs. Their opposed interpretations of the situation have constituted genuinely rival assertions, whose assertion-status has the peculiar characteristic of being guaranteed retrospectively by a future crux.[1]

One may now turn one's attention to comparable Jaina ideas on this point. The first of these is provided by the doctrine of the *pañca-parameṣṭhins:* "the five kinds of persons worshipped by the Jains as representing the ideal in life at the different stages of realization".[2] Only the first two need detain us here:

---

1. John H. Hick, *op. cit.*, p. 104-105.
2. Hiralal Jain, "Jainism: Its history, Principles, and Precepts", in Haridas Bhattacharyya, ed., *op. cit.*, Vol. I, p. 418.

> Thus, according to Jainism, there is no creation of the world, nor is there any Creator necessary to explain the nature of the world. After completely conquering all the *karmas* and destroying all the shackles of *sāmsāric* (worldly) consequences, the Self exists in its supreme purity as *siddha-parameṣṭhin*, endowed with the qualities of infinite perception, infinite knowledge, infinite bliss, and infinite power. This *parameṣṭhin* with infinite qualities is the conqueror of *samsāra*, is the *jina*, and he serves as the ideal to be aimed at by all persons who desire to escape form the cycle of births and deaths characteristic of *samsāra*.
>
> Besides the *siddha-parameṣṭhin*, Jainism recognizes the arhatparameṣṭhin, who represents a lower stage in liberation than the *siddha-parameṣṭhin*. Nevertheless, in some respects, the stage of *arhat* shoulsd be considered important from the human point of view, because it is in this stage of Arhathood that the *arhat* or tīrthankara reveals, for the benefit of the world, the path to salvation and all the various Āgamas or scriptures describing such a path.[1]

Moreover, Jaina literature provides its own parable to go with the one developed by Professor John Hick. It is the famous parable of the Man in the Well. The account presented below is from Samarādityakathā of Haribhadra (seventh century).

> A certain man, much oppressed by the woes of poverty,
> Left his own home, and set out for another country.
> He passed through the land, with its villages, cities, and harbors,
> And after a few days he lost his way.
>
> And he came to a forest, thick with trees—and full of wild beasts.There, while he was stumbling over the rugged paths,—a prey to thirst and hunger, he saw a mad elephant, fiercely trumpeting, charging him with upraised trunk. At the same time there appeared before him a most evil demoness, holding a sharp sword, dreadful in face and form, and laughing with loud and shrill laughter. Seeing them he trembled in all his limbs with deathly

1. *Ibid.*, p. 415-416.

fear, and looked in all directions. There, to the east of him, he saw a great banyan tree—

And he ran quickly and reached the mighty tree.
But his spirits fell, for it was so high that even the birds could not fly over it,
And he could not climb its high unscalable trunk...
All his limbs trembled with terrible fear,
Until, looking round, he saw nearby an old well covered with grass.
Afraid of death, craving to live if only a moment longer,
He flung himself into the well at the foot of the banyan tree.
A clump of reeds grew from its deep wall, and to this he clung,
While below him he saw terrible snakes, enraged at the sound of his falling;
And at the very bottom, known from the hiss of its breath, was a black and mighty python
With mouth agape, its body thick as the trunk of a heavenly elephant, with terrible red eyes.
He thought, "My life will only last as long as these reeds hold fast,"
And he raised his head; and there, on the clump of reeds, he saw two large mice,
One white, one black, their sharp teeth ever gnawing at the roots of the reed-clump.
Then up came the wild elephant, and, enraged the more at not catching him,
Charged time and again at the trunk of the banyan tree
Which hung over the old well, shook loose and fell.

The man's whole body was stung by a swarm of angry bees,
But, just by chance, a drop of honey fell on his head,
Rolled down his brow, and somehow reached his lips,
And gave him a moment's sweetness. He longed for other drops,
And he thought nothing of the python, the snakes, the elephant, the mice, the well, or the bees,
In his excited craving for yet more drops of honey.
This parable is powerful to clear the minds of those on the way to freedom.

Now hear its sure interpretation.

The man is the soul, his wandering in the forest the four types of existence.

The wild elephant is death, the demoness old age.

The banyan tree is salvation, where there is no fear of death, the elephant,

But which no sensual man can climb.

The well is human life, the snakes are passions,

Which so overcome a man that he does not know what he should do.

The tuft of reed is man's allotted span, during which the soul exists embodied;

The mice which steadily gnaw it are the dark and bright fortnights.

The stinging bees are manifold diseases,

Which torment a man until he has not a moment's joy.

The awful python is hell, seizing the man bemused by sensual pleasure,

Fallen in which the soul suffers pains by the thousand.

The drops of honey are trivial pleasures, terrible at the last.

How can a wise man want them, in the midst of such peril and hardship?[1]

The point regarding the *parameṣṭhins* may be developed along two lines. The first is that God is seen in Christian thought as out there looking out for the devotee, but in Jainism "All Tīrthankaras

---

1. Wm Theodore de Bary, ed., *op. cit.*, Vol. I, pp. 53-55. Some abridged English accounts are also presented below since each conveys it own flavour. (1) "Thus for the Jain, even more perhaps than for the Buddhist, the universe is a place of utter misery and sorrow, and its few moments of happiness in no way compensate for the essential horror of existence. The pessimism of the Jain outlook is nowhere better expressed than in a famous parable, 'The Man in the Well'. A traveller was journeying through a dense and wild forest when he encountered a mad elephant which charged him with upraised trunk. As he turned to flee, a terrible demoness with a naked sword in her hand appeared before him and barred his path. There was a great tree near the track, and he ran up to it, hoping to find safety in its branches, but he could find no foothold in its smooth trunk. His only refuge was an old well, covered with grass and weeds, at the foot of the tree, and into this he leapt.

have reached moksa at their death, and they neither care for nor have any influence on worldly affairs; but yet they are regarded

As he fell he managed to catch hold of a clump of reeds which grew from the wall, and there he hung, midway between the mouth of the well and its bottom. Looking down, he saw that the bottom did not contain water, but was surrounded by snakes, which hissed at him as he hung above them. In their midst was a might python, its mouth agape, waiting to catch him when he fell. Raising his head again, the man saw on the clump of reeds two mice, one white and the other black, busily gnawing away at the roots. Meanwhile the wild elephant ran up to the well, and, enraged at losing its victim, began charging at the trunk of the tree. Thus he dislodged a honeycomb which hung from a branch above the well, and it fell upon the man hanging there so precariously. Angry bees swarmed round his head and tormented him with their stings. But one drop of honey fell on his brow, rolled down his face and reached his lips. Immediately he forgot his peril and thought of nothing more than of obtaining another drop of honey.

The main purport of this story is quite obvious, but the Jain finds a parallel to each of the many horrors which beset the unfortunate traveller. The man, of course, is the soul, and his journey through the forest is *saṁsāra*. The elephant represents death; the demoness, old age. The tree is the way to salvation, which the ordinary man cannot climb. The well is human life, the snakes are passions, the python is hell. The tuft of reed is man's allotted span, and the black and white mice are the dark and bright halves of the month. The bees are diseases and troubles, while the honey, of course, represents the trivial pleasures of our earthly existence (*Samarāicca-Kahā*, ii. 55-80). Whether or not he taste a few more drops of honey, at last the mice will do their work and the man will fall into the jaws of the python. But her the analogy breaks down, for the python of hell must sooner or later disgorge the man and return him to the forest of the world, only to suffer further terrors of a like kind". (A.L. Basham, "Jainism" in R.C. Zaehner, ed., *op cit.*, p. 263). (2) "A well-known story depicts the precarious state of a soul falling into deeper layers of bondage. The story represents a soul as a human being who falls into a well. He clutches the branch of a tree that is growing form the side of the well to save himself from falling deeper. As he hangs on, he sees two mice, one black and one white, gnawing at the branch. He realizes that when the mice chew through the wood, he will fall. Glancing at the pit under him he sees poisonous serpents waiting for him. At this moment a beehive on the tree above shakes a bit and drops of honey fall near the man. Forgetting his predicament, he reaches out for the honey and loses his grip of the branch just to have the fleeting sense of enjoyment.

The man in the well is the soul, which can at any moment fall into deeper trouble. The mice represent our lives: the white mouse symbolizes the days and the black mouse the nights. Time is eating away at our lives. And yet, instead of concentrating our energies in getting out of the problems that we find ourselves in, we try to experience a fleeting sense of enjoyment, even at the cost of out ultimate happiness. If one loses one's chance to get onto the right path, one is reborn again and yet again. But the situation of the as 'Gods' by the Jains and are worshipped".[1] The second is that one of the problems the theist might face is: (a) How does one know that God is God and (b) How does one know that it is the Christian God. As John Hick notes: "Even if it were granted (as of course many philosophers would not be willing to grant) that it makes sense to speak of continued personal existence after death, an experience of survival would not necessarily serve to verify theism. It might be taken as just a surprising natural fact. The deceased atheist able to remember life on earth might find that the universe has turned out to be more complex, and perhaps more to be approved of, than he or she had realized. However, the mere fact of survival, with a new body in a new environment, would not by itself demonstrate to such a person the reality of God. The life to come might turn out to be as religiously ambiguous as this present life. It might still be quite unclear whether or not there is a God".[2] According to John Hick question (b) is more easily answered than question (a) because "Although it is difficult to say what future experiences would verify theism in general, it is less difficult to say what would verify the more specific claims of such a religion as Christianity, with its own built-in eschatological beliefs. The system of ideas that surrounds the Christian concept of God, and in the light of which that concept has to be understood, includes expectations concerning the final fulfillment of God's purpose for humanity in the 'Kingdom of God.' The experience that would verify Christian belief in God is the experience of participating in that eventual fulfillment".[3]

---

man in the well is not entirely hopeless. He is not destined necessarily to revolve endlessly in the cycle of birth and death". (Vasudha Narayaṇan, *op. cit.*, p. 153-154).

1. Surendranath Dasgupta, *op. cit.*, Vol. I, p. 169-170.
2. John H. Hick, *op. cit.*, p. 105.
3. *Ibid.* He goes on to say (*Ibid.*): "According to the new Testament, the general nature of God's purpose for human life is the creation of 'children of God' who shall participate in eternal life. One can say this much without professing advance knowledge of the concrete forms of such a fulfillment. The situation is analogous to that of a small child looking forward to adult life and then, having grown to adulthood, looking back upon childhood. The child possesses and can use correctly the concept of "being grown-up," although, as a child, one does not yet know what it is like to be grown-up. When one reaches adulthood, one is, nevertheless, able to know that one has reached

These problems are unlikely to arise in the Jaina case of eschatological verification. First of all, the problem of knowing God would not arise, as there is no God. Of course, if the Jaina being does encounter God in a post-mortem existence, then it would create a problem for Jaina philosophy, but of a different kind being addressed at the moment. Next, the problem of knowing whether the Jaina has reached the Jaina version of the "Beatific Vision" would not arise, as there are clear criteria supplied for it. This specification is spatial both in terms of *where* one is and the *form* in which one is present there.

> Souls in this final abode (referred to as Īsat–Prāgbhāra-bhūmi, "the slightly bending place," because of its domelike appearance) are thought by Jainas to possess a definite shape. This shape is identical to that of the last incarnation, though on a slightly reduced scale (the empty spaces found in an earthly body are no longer present). No clear explanation is offered for this seeming association of the totally liberated soul with its former condition. We can only surmise that, in addition to preserving the individuality of siddhas in the state of mokṣa where all souls are otherwise of identical nature, such a concept serves to emphasize the fact that every siddha was previously an ordinary human being; hence the Jaina aspirant will be encouraged to pursue the path of purification ever more rigorously, for he will be reminded that even the most exalted souls were once trapped in bondage just as he is now.[1]

---

it, for one's understanding of adult maturity grows as one matures. Something analogous may be supposed to happen in the case of the fulfillment of the divine purpose for human life, That fulfillment may be as far removed from our present condition as is mature adulthood from the mind of a little child. Indeed, it may be much further removed; but we already possess some notion of it (given in the person of Christ), and as we move toward it our concept will thereby become more adequate. If and when we finally reach that fulfillment, the problem of recognizing it will have disappeared in the process."

1. Padmanabh S. Jaini, *The Jaina Path of Purification*, p. 270, emphasis added. He supplies the following attempts at explanation in a footnote (*Ibid.*, p. 270 note 37):

   This rather dramatic departure from the realm of embodiment is sometimes explained as due to an "inherent tendency" of the soul to "break away

Padmanabha S. Jaini does hasten to add:

> But again, it must be borne in mind that any description of the perfected being, or of the infinite cognition and bliss which characterize him is purely conventional. In reality such things, lying as they do beyond the space-time limitations of ordinary human consciousness, cannot be described at all.[1]

One might, however, wish to ask a somewhat different but not unrelated question: how does the Jaina Arhat know that he (or she)[2] has realized Arhathood? Arhathood is characterized by omniscience so the Arhat would presumably know everything, which would include the knowledge of not only all that is known but also the knowledge that all is known.[3]

Existence, Factity and Reality

The chapter started with a discussion of the idea of a veracious statement and how the philosophical pursuit of it led to concepts of verifiable and falsifiable statements. When this pursuit was allied with Christian theism, it gave rise to the concept of eschatological verification. It will be recalled that it was the concept of "making a difference", or more properly, "making an experienceable difference", which started one out on the logical positivist road. It might not be irrelevant to ask how this new condition affects our more commonplace understanding of such expressions as God exists, God's existence is a fact or that God is real. According to John Hick:

---

from" or "rise above" all karmas. Alternatively, its arrow-like flight to the summit of the universe is ascribed to "momentum" originally set up by the bodily activities; a similar phenomenon occurs, we are told, when the potters's wheel continues to rotate long after the potter has ceased to turn it.

It is interesting that the first is often compared with the upward movement of a flame which is reminiscent of Buddha's comparison of the Arhat's *after his final passing* away with that of fire; while the latter is reminiscent of the Hindu explanation of how a liberated one *continues to live on the earth even after having* become liberated.

1. *Ibid.*, p. 270.
2. See Padmanabh S. Jaini, *Gender and Salvation: Jaina Debates on the Spiritual Liberation of Women* (Berkeley: University of California Press, 1991).
3. However, see B.K. Matilal, *op. cit.*, p. 24.

> A suggestion that coheres with the idea of eschatological verification is that the common core to the concepts of "existence," fact," and "reality" is the idea of "making a difference." To say that *x* exists or is real, that it is a fact that there is an *x*, is to claim that the character of the universe differs in some specific way from the character that *an x*-less universe would have. The nature of this difference will naturally depend upon the character of the *x* in question, and the meaning of "God exists" will be indicated by spelling out the past, present, and future difference which God's existence is alleged to make within human experience.[1]

The issue is faced by Jaina philosophy in reverse. It is not one of making a difference but what one makes of the difference which characterises this plural world. This change in perspective has important consequences for how existence, factity and reality are conceived in Jainism.

1. *Ibid.*, p. 107-108.

CHAPTER IX

THE PROBLEM OF RELIGIOUS PLURALISM

Many Faiths

The fact of religious plurality is hard to escape in the world in which we live. In order to experience the full force of the problem:

> The problem can be posed very concretely in this way. If I had been born in India, I would probably be a Hindu; if in Egypt, probably a Muslim; if in Sri Lanka, probably a Buddhist; but I was born in England and am, predictably, a Christian. (Of course, a different "I" would have developed in each case.) These different religions seem to say different and incompatible things about the nature of ultimate reality, about the modes of divine activity, and about the nature and destiny of the human race. Is the divine nature personal or nonpersonal? Does deity become incarnate in the world? Are human beings reborn again and again on earth? Is the empirical self the real self, destined for eternal life in fellowship with God, or is it only a temporary and illusory manifestation of an eternal higher self? Is the Bible, or the Qur'an, or the Bhagavad Gita the Word of God? If what Christianity says in answer to such questions is true, must not what Hinduism says be to a large extent false? If what Buddhism says is true, must not what Islam says be largely false?[1]

The reader will notice that Jainism is not mentioned in this passage at all. This is not surprising for Jainism as a religion is perhaps more known for its antiquity than its popularity. In a sense, however, this neglect is unfortunate. Jainism is an immensely rich philosophical resource for addressing the question of the

1. John H. Hick, *op. cit.*, p. 109-110.

conflicting truth claims of different religions. To give credence to this statement, we may draw on two features of this religious plurality, one historical, the other philosophical, which are usually identified as starting points for the discussion of the subject on hand.

Historically, the point is often made that the major religions of the world evolved in relative, if majestic, isolation over the centuries. It is the globalization of the world, and the movement of the world from being a 'global village' towards becoming a 'global city' (given the accelerating rate of urbanization) which has made the problems, raised by the conflicting truth claims of the major religions, acute. The statement is no doubt true, though it might understate the extent of camouflaged interaction which did go on among the various religions in the past. Jainism reminds us of this fact, for only recently has Jainism gone international and thus emerged as a player in its own right on the international religious arena. The point to note here is that even in this process, its first shot at global participation was an ecumenical one. Swami Vivekananda's presence at the World Parliament of Religions in 1893 is well known for inaugurating a Hindu presence in the West. It is not as well known that, at that Parliament, the most learned paper on Hinduism was delivered by a Jaina scholar, who had prepared assiduously for the occasion years in advance. This fact in itself gives us reason for pause. It should make us think, or at least wonder, if a part, even a good part, of the coming clash of religions might not involve some tilting at windmills! And as a matter of historical interest we might wish to consider two other points: the Jaina insistence that the Jainas preserve an attitude of impartiality towards their *own* teachers and the Jaina willingness to admit that non-Jainas can achieve liberation, without having to convert to Jainism. That this goes beyond the popular understanding of the "anonymous Christian" will become obvious later. For the moment it should suffice to cite the prooftexts for the two claims just made.

> I have no bias for Mahāvīra, and none *against* Kapila and others. *Reasonable words alone are acceptable* to me, whosoever's they might be.[1]

x x x

1. Maibhadra, as cited by S. Chatterjee and D. Datta, *An Introduction to Indian Philosophy* (Calcutta: University of Calcutta, 1968) p. 105.

> No matter whether he is a Svetāmbara or a Digambara [two Jaina sects], a Buddhist or a follower of any other creed, one who has realised the self-sameness of the soul, i.e. looks on all creatures as his own self, attains salvation.[1]

The discussion of the conflicting claims of religions is often also introduced with a philosophical consideration. It is asserted, for instance, that the plurality of religions undermines the validity of each religion, and even of religion itself, hopelessly.

> The skeptical thrust of these questions goes very deep; for it is a short step from the thought that different religions cannot all be true, although they each claim to be, to the thought that in all probability none of them is true. Thus Hume laid down the principle "that, in matters of religion, whatever is different is contrary; and that it is impossible the religions of ancient Rome, of Turkey, of Siam, and of China should, all of them, be established on any solid foundation." Accordingly, regarding miracles as evidence for the truth of a particular faith, "Every miracle, therefore, pretended to have been wrought in any of these religions (and all of them abound in miracles), as its direct scope is to establish the particular religion to which it is attributed; so has it the same force, though more indirectly, to overthrow every other system." By the same reasoning, any ground for believing a particular religion to be true must operate as a ground for believing every other religion to be false; accordingly, for any particular religion there will always be far more reason for believing it to be false than for believing it to be true. This is the skeptical argument that arises from the conflicting truth claims of the various world faiths.[2]

The point, of course, possesses considerable force, but has less impact if buffered by Jaina philosophy. In this case we should place

1. Ratnaśekhara, as cited by S. Radhakrishnan, *op. cit.*, Vol. I, p. 328. The self-sameness of the soul as mentioned should not be confused with the Hindu identity of Brahman=Ātman.
2. John H. Hick, *op. cit.*, p. 10.

the views of the Jaina philosopher Siddhasena alongside those of Hume. He observes:

> All the standpoint (*nayas*) are right in their own respective spheres but if they are taken to be refutations, each of the other, then they are wrong. But a man who knows the 'non-one-sided' nature of reality never says that a particular view is absolutely wrong.[1]

Professor B.K. Matilal has even suggested that "on rare occasions even the famous Buddhist thinker Nāgārjuna "seems to betray what may be called the Jaina spirit of concession and neutrality",[2] as in the following verse of Madhyamkakārikā (18.8):

> Everything is true; not everything is true; both, everything is true, and not everything is true; or, neither everything is true nor is everything not true. This is the teaching of the Buddha.[3]

It could, of course, be argued that this spirit of accommodation is Indic in nature. After all, does it not speak of Hindu tolerance that it should allow the Hindu tradition to be presented at the World Parliament of Religions by a Jaina? And the above statement of Nāgārjuna could also be seen as a specific example of a larger catholicity which characterises all religions of Indian origin. This may be so but it misses the important point that in the Jaina case this attitude is grounded in a *philosophical* doctrine.[4] We shall have occasion to revert to this point later. In the meantime it is worth noting that the evidence from Jainism also helps to draw attention to the subtle ways in which the various religious traditions did interact. Wilfred Cantwell Smith has drawn attention to the world wide circulation of a certain parable in religious circles.[5] One gathers from the *Confessions* of Tolstoy that one particular fable acted as a catalyst in his life. "In this tale, the human condition

1. Cited by B.K. Matilal, *op. cit.*, p. 31.
2. *Ibid.*
3. Cited, *Ibid.*
4. *Ibid.*, p. 6.
5. Wilfred Cantwell Smith, *Towards a World Theology: Faith and the Comparative History of Religion* (Philadelphia: The Westminster Press, 1981) Chapter I.

is portrayed as like that of a man who, fleeing from a furious beast, falls into a well and is held from dropping into the jaws of a devouring dragon below only by clinging to a bush that will, he sees, presently inevitably give way, since it is being nibbled at by two mice, one white and one black, that go round and round and slowly but relentlessly gnaw at its roots. The two mice are day and night; the bush, which tastes sweet at first but soon loses its savour, is one's worldly position; man knows that he or she must in due course die."[1]

Wilfred Cantwell Smith goes on to show how this parable was disseminated in the Christian world.[2] It entered the Christian West through an Arabic version,[3] which had its origin in a Buddhist account[4], and the Buddhists "picked it up for incorporation from either a Hindu or a Jaina source".[5] To complete the circle, as it were, Tolstoy influenced Gandhi profoundly.[6] Even if the story does not figure in this last link, "it is entrancing to discover that Tolstoi, in nineteenth-century Russia, had his spiritual life given shape by a story which we can trace from the Jains, and perhaps from pre-Sanskritic India".[7] In his notes, interestingly, Professor Smith alludes to the very source from which it was cited in an earlier chapter.[8]

The Concept of Religion

Some scholars have suggested that at least part of the problem with the conflicting truth claims of religion is the term religion itself. Wilfred Cantwell Smith argues that it is an artificial intellectual construct which reifies the actual religious life of the people. He proposes that "the word [religion], and the concepts should be

1. *Ibid.*, p. 7.
2. *Ibid.*, p. 8.
3. *Ibid.*
4. *Ibid.*, p. 9.
5. *Ibid.*, p. 9.
6. *Ibid.*, p. 10-11.
7. *Ibid.*, p. 10.
8. *Ibid.*, p. 197 note 12. I have encountered a Hindu version putatively from the Mahābhārata.

dropped in all but the first, personalist sense [faith]"[1], and goes on to say

> I ask whether these studies may not proceed more satisfactorily in future if, putting aside the concept 'religion' or 'the religions' to describe the two, we elect to work rather with two separate concepts.
>
> I propose to call these 'cumulative tradition', on the one hand, and 'faith', on the other. the link between the two is the living person.
>
> By 'faith' I mean personal faith. I shall endeavour to elucidate this in our next chapter. For the moment let it stand for an inner religious experience or involvement of a particular person; the impingement on him of the transcendent, putative or real. By 'cumulative tradition' I mean the entire mass of overt objective data that constitutes the historical deposit, as it were, of the past religious life of the community in question: temples, scriptures, theological systems, dance patterns, legal and other social institutions, conventions, moral codes, myths, and so on; anything that can be and is transmitted from one person, one generation, to another, and that a historian can observe.[2]

How could one react to this proposal from the perspective of Jaina philosophy? One way of responding to it would be the following. If we apply the Jaina doctrine of Sevenfold Viewpoints to it, the following seven understandings of the term might be generated. (1) *Naīgamanaya*: that religion is both a universal and a personal category; (2) *Sangrahanaya*: that every human being in the world has a religion; (3) *Vyavaharanaya*: that every human being has his or her own religion; (4) *Ṛjusūtranaya*: what is his religion right now? (5) *Śabdanaya*: what is his or her religion; (6) *Samabhirūdhanaya*: he or she subscribes to a religion and (7) *Evambhūtanaya*: religion binds him or her to God or reality.

---

1. Wilfred Cantwell Smith, *The Meaning and End of Religion* (New York: The Macmillan Company, 1963) p. 50-57.
2. *Ibid.*, p. 156-157.

The result is interesting: the first four understanding veer towards the 'cumulative tradition' understanding of religion; the last four towards the 'faith' understanding and the radical separation of the two is avoided in the synthetic hands of Jaina epistemology.

Towards a Solution

John H. Hick identifies three main factors which, in his opinion, aggravate the difficulties caused by the conflicting truth claims of world religions: "we may distinguish three aspects of this question: differences in modes of experiencing the divine reality; differences of philosophical and theological theory concerning that reality or concerning the implications of religious experience; and differences in the key or revelatory experiences that unify a stream of religious life."[1]

In the case of the first category, Hick distinguishes between the personal and nonpersonal modes of apprehending reality and proposes that they could be considered different and not necessarily contrary; and the case of the second category, he regards as sufficiently fluid and flexible as not to pose serious problems. His gravest reservations are about the third category. In his view, because each major religious tradition "has its holy founder or scripture, or both, in which the divine reality has been revealed"[2], this third category represents the most difficult area of accommodation.

The history of Jainism sheds interesting light on the question. First of all, the entire Jaina canon did not receive definitive form until the fifth century CE, while tradition goes back at least to sixth century BCE, if not earlier.[3] Then the two main sects, the Digambara and the Śvetāmbara "differ over how later texts might reflect or preserve what is supposed to have been in the pūrvas",[4] the lost pristine texts, and the two sects also "hold different books as sacred".[5] Thus the "scripture" need not prove such an obstacle in this case.

1. John H. Hick, *op. cit.*, p. 115.
2. *Ibid.*, p. 116.
3. M. Hiriyanna, *Outlines of Indian Philosophy*, p. 155.
4. Vasudha Narayanan, *op. cit.*, p. 146-147.
5. *Ibid.*

However, while Buddhism did not, at least not as a monastic order, retain its individuality in India, Jainism "has continued to retain its individuality to this day, owing chiefly to its conservatism, 'to its scrupulous care for the preservation of ancient customs, institutions and doctrines'."[1] Moreover, the Jaina doctrines themselves might provide a framework of their own for addressing the problems raised by the conflicting truth claims of world religions, and it is to a consideration of these that we now turn.

Prior to undertaking such a step, however, it might be wise to examine Professor John Hick's solution to the problem in the light of Jainism.

John Hick uses the distinction drawn by Kant "between the world as it is *an sich*, which he called the noumenal world, and world as it appears to human consciousness, which he called the phenomenal world".[2] John Hick proposes that we apply a similar framework to our experience of the ultimate reality, distinguishing between what it might be in itself and how it is experienced by us. He writes:

> Is it possible to adopt the broad Kantian distinction between the world as it is in itself and the world as it appears to us with our particular cognitive machinery, and apply it to the relation between the Ultimate Reality and our different human awareness of that Reality? If so, we shall think in terms of a single divine noumenon and many diverse divine phenomena. We may form the hypothesis that the Real *an sich* is experienced by human beings in terms of one of two basic religious concepts. One is the concept of God, or of the Real experienced as personal, which presides over the theistic forms of religion. The other is the concept of the Absolute, or of the Real experienced as nonpersonal, which presides over the various nontheistic forms of religion.[3]

1. M. Hiriyanna, *Essentials of Indian Philosophy*, p. 60.
2. John H. Hick, *op. cit.*, p. 118. The Kantian distinction does find an echo in the distinction drawn between *pramāna* and *naya* in Jain epistemology, where *pramāna* denotes "knowledge of a thing as it is in itself" and *naya* "knowledge of a thing it its relation" (S. Radhakrishnan, *op. cit.*, Vol. I, p. 298.
3. John H. Hick *op. cit.*, p. 118.

John Hick argues his case persuasively and concludes that "it is a possible, and indeed an attractive hypothesis as an alternative to total skepticism that the great religious traditions of the world represent different human perceptions of and response to the same infinite divine Reality."[1]

The basic difficulty this presents in the case of Jainism is that Jainism does not postulate any such infinite divine reality. It denies a single divine noumenon. It also denies both personal and nonpersonal divine phenomenon.[2] It provides for the salvation for the individual and that salvation is open to all. It therefore provides a soteriological rather than an ontological basis for meeting the conflicting truth claims. But most scholars have argued that Jainism's most promising contribution in this context might lie in the direction of providing an epistemological framework for reconciling the conflicting truth claims of religions.

Difference Between Buddhist and Jaina Approaches

John Hick proposes his scheme as an alternative to 'total skepticism'. This provides a useful point of entry into the scene in ancient India, which in the sixth century BCE was, by all accounts, characterised by unprecedented religious ferment[3] or what we would, in contemporary idiom, dub as a pluralist bazaar. The wide differences in religious opinions had the predictable effect of turning some intellectually sensitive people into agnostics. One of them, Sañjaya, is well known.[4] The following statement is attributed to him:

> 'If you ask me whether there is future existence (*atthi paraloko*) well, if I believed that there was, I should say so. But I do not say so. And I do not say it is thus or this. And I do not say it is otherwise, and I do not say that it is not so, nor do I say it is not not so. If you ask me whether there is no future existence (*na'tthi paraloko*), well, if I believed...If

1. *Ibid.*, p. 119.
2. See S. Radhakrishnan, *op. cit.*, Vol. I, p. 312, 329, 338.
3. Wm. Theodore de Bary, ed., *op. cit.*, Vol. I, pp. 39-44.
4. Pandit N. Aiyaswami Sastri, "Śramaa or Non-Brāhmanical Sects", in Haridas Bhattacharyya, ed., *op. cit.*, Vol. I, p. 399.

you ask me whether there neither is nor is not another world (*n'ev'atthi no na'tthi paraloko*), well, if I believed...'

B.K. Matilal has contrasted the attitudes adopted by Buddha and Mahāvīra in the face of similar questions. He remarks:

> Mahāvīra thus developed a philosophy of synthesis and toleration, which later came to be designated as the *anekānta-*vāda. The Buddha's method was one of withdrawal from philosophic disputes, for he avoided committing himself to any extreme view. But Mahāvīra's method was one of commitment, for he attempted to understand the points of view of the fighting parties (in a philosophic dispute) so that their dispute could be resolved and reconciled. Thus, the essence of the anekānta-vāda lies in exposing and making explicit the standpoint or presuppositions of different philosophic schools.[1]

The doctrine of *anekāntavāda* has been already alluded to. In relation to it Professor B.K. Matilal makes the plausible suggestion that we should distinguish between two versions of it. "The term is used, in the first place, to denote the Jaina metaphysical doctine, by which I mean the Jaina view of reality. Roughly, the Jainas believe that reality is manifold and each entity has a manifold nature, consists of diverse forms and modes, of innumerable aspects. In this sense, therefore, the term can correctly be translated as 'the theory of manifoldness of reality'", and as such has been examined in an earlier chapter. Professor Matilal then goes on to point out, however, that "the term '*anekānta-vāda*' is also used for the Jaina philosophic method–as a method which allows for reconciliation, integration, and synthesis of conflicting philosophic views".[2]

One component of the doctrine of *anekāntavāda* is *nyavāda* or the doctrine of standpoint. Jaina thinkers have used this doctrine

1. B.K. Matilal, *op. cit.*, p. 23.
2. *Ibid.*, p. 25. He also adds: "In this sense, the *anekānta-vāda* is the proper heir to the *vibhajya-vāda* of *Mahāvira*".

single system. The four *nayas* or standpoint may briefly be summarized for convenience as follows:

> When we take a co-ordinated view of things, we are said to be resorting to *naigama naya*. When we are inclined towards generalization, it is *saṅgraha naya*; and when inclined towards particularization, it is *vyavahāra naya*. When a specific point or period of time is of the essence, it is *jusūtra naya*.[1]

The Jainas hold that "the Nyāya-Vaiśesika, the Vedānta, the Sāmkhya and the Buddhist, have each tried to interpret and systematize experience from one of the above four points of view [in that order]".[2] However, having lost sight of this fact, "each regards the interpretation from his point of view absolutely true to the exclusion of other points of view"[3] and thus becomes one-sided in its approach to reality.

In a somewhat similar way, a framework could be provided for accommodating diverse views on the existence and relationship of the universals and the particulars in its scheme of standpoint. Thus: "Sāmkhya and Advaita Vedānta deny *viśesas* [particulars], while Buddhism denies sāmānya [universal]. *Nyāya-Vaiśesika* accepts both, and looks upon the concrete thing as a complex make up of the universal and the particular. But Jainism considers the distinction to be a relative one, while *Nyāya-Vaiśesika* looks upon it as absolute".[4] The fact that the Jaina position could be included *within it* augurs well for its universality and versatility.

Further Comments

Although we have been led to an epistemology of religious pluralism by the ontology of Jainism, perhaps it is not necessary to

1. Hiralal Jain, "Jainism: Its History, Principles and Precepts, *op. cit.*, p. 406.
2. Surendranath Dasgupta, *op. cit.*, Vol. I, p. 178. Also see pages 177-178. S. Radhakrishnan (*op. cit.*, Vol. I, p. 301) offers a slightly different pairing: "According to the Jains, the Nyāya-Vaiśesika, the Sāmkhya, the Advaita Vedānta and the Buddhist systems adopt the first four nayas respectively and mistake them for the whole truth". For a somewhat different view see B.K. Matilal, *op. cit.*, p.34.
3. Surendranath Dasgupta, *op. cit.*, Vol. I, p. 178.
4. S. Radhakrishnan, *op. cit.*, Vol. I, p. 300.

ralism by the ontology of Jainism, perhaps it is not necessary to believe in Jaina ontology to benefit from its epistemology. As B.K. Matilal points out:

> The philosophic position of the Jainas in this way found expression in the *anekānta* doctrine, a doctrine that was characterized by toleration, understanding and respect for the views of others. This is a unique character of Jaina philosophy and religion, which I find most [admirable]. For, very seldom [has] such a sincere attempt been made to understand the position of the adversary. Whether the fundamental assumption of ontology (i. e., the thesis that reality is many-sided or things are basically of inifinitefold nature) is correct or not, is another matter. But certainly the professed catholicity of the Jaina outlook (an attitude which the early Jesuits shared, perhaps, from a different motivation) can hardly be denied.[1]

It is also worth noting, in conclusion, that the "prophets" of Jainism are called *tīrthankaras.* Although the word is usually translated as "ford-makers",[2] the term has more recently been translated as 'bridge-builders'.[3] Is it too much to expect that this translation might convey a hint of the role Jainism is destined to play in the context of the conflicting truth-claims of religions?

1. B.K. Matilal, *op. cit.*, p. 6.
2. A.L. Basham, *The Wonder That Was India*, p. 288.
3. Vasudha Narayanan, *op. cit.*, p. 136.

CHAPTER X

HUMAN DESTINY: WESTERN PERSPECTIVES

The Body–Soul Distinction

It is a fact of some, or perhaps even considerable interest that human beings, from very early on in the history of human consciousness, began to make a distinction which roughly corresponds to what later came to be known as the body-soul distinction.[1] This is historically suggested by the manner in which early burials were undertaken.[2] It is also surmised anthropologically that early experiences of seeing one's shadow, or the deceased one's in dreams, may have encouraged this belief.[3] There is every reason to believe that "some kind of distinction between physical body and immaterial or semimaterial soul seems to be as old as human culture".[4]

India is among the older cradles of human culture, and, among the religions of Indian origin, a hoary antiquity can be claimed for Jainism.[5] In any case "the primitive heritage of Jainism is very evident"[6] to scholars like A.L. Basham. He also speculates that it were these "primitive animistic ideas" which are responsible for the Jaina beliefs, which attribute life to a wide variety of entities and objects.

From a philosophical point of view, Jainism is of interest here

1. Bruce Lincoln, "Human Body", in Mircea Eliade, Editor in Chief, *The Encyclopedia of Religion* (New York: Macmillan Publishing Company, 1987) Vol. 6, p. 499-500.
2. See Johannes Maringer, The Gods of Prehistoric Man (New York: Knopf, 1960).
3. See E.E. Evans-Pritchard, *Theories of Primitive Religion* (Oxford: Clarendon Press, 1965).
4. John H. Hick, *op. cit.*, p. 120.
5. A.N. Upadhye, *op. cit.*, p. 100-101.
6. A.L. Basham, "Jainism", in R.C. Zaehner, ed., *op. cit.*, p. 262.

on account of its antiquity, vouched for by other sources, which brings it in line with Western views regarding the evolution of religious ideas.[1] What is of even more interest, however, is the comprehensiveness of the co-existence of the matter-soul distinction in Jainism. Whereas the body-soul distinction is normally restricted to human beings, or at best extended to animals in most religions, according to Jainism even "atoms or aggregates of them are supposed to harbour souls so that the whole universe may be said to be throbbing with life".[2] This fact has important eschatological implications at the cosmic level,[3] though one must now turn away from that issue to the question of human destiny.

The Immortality of the Soul

Plato (428/7- 348/7 BCE) is said to have "systematically developed the body-mind dichotomy" and to have "first attempted to prove the immortality of the soul".[4] He achieved this result in two ways. One way in which this result was achieved was by assigning the body and the "intellect" to two distinct realms, one changing and the other unchanging. The body belonged to the former, the intellect to the latter, which was inhabited by universals such as "goodness", as opposed to things which were merely good. Thus in the Platonic vision, "being related to this higher and abiding realm rather than to the evanescent world of sense, the soul is immortal. Hence, one who devotes one's life to the contemplation of eternal realities rather than to the gratification of the fleeting desires of the body will find at death that whereas the body turns to death, one's soul gravitates to the realm of the unchanging, there to live forever".[5]

There are some broad similarities between the Platonic and Jaina visions. In Plato, eternal life results from being freed from the toils of matter. This is also true in Jainism, but with this difference that, in Jainism, freedom from material bonds does not presuppose the dissolution of the body. Such a state of sancti-

1. A.N. Upadhye, *op. cit.*, p. 100. Note the reference to animism.
2. M. Hiriyanna, *The Essentials of Indian Philosophy*, p. 62.
3. Padmanabh S. Jaini, "Karma and the Problem of Rebirth in Jainism", *op. cit.*, p. 224ff.
4. John H. Hick, *op. cit.*, p. 120.
5. John H. Hick, *op. cit.*, p. 120-121.

fication can be achieved in a pre-mortem state in Jainism. The idea of liberated beings ascending to a realm where they dwell in beatitude is also present in Jainism in its concept of the śiddhaśilā, a place where the liberated souls abide. However, even in the state of liberation, the soul possesses size.[1] The Jainas, moreover, do not associate universals alone with reality. Whereas, according to Plato, only the permanent substratum can be real, according to Jainism "origination and destruction relate to modes of reality; and permanence to their substratum".[2] Reality encompasses both dimensions.

We may now examine the second argument Plato offers for establishing the immortality of the soul. This is the famous argument that only objects which are composite are liable to destruction and the soul, being impartite, is imperishable. This argument was destined to become standard in Western thought and was developed by Jacques Maritain as follows:

> A spiritual soul cannot be corrupted, since it possesses no matter; it cannot be disintegrated, since it has no substantial parts; it cannot lose its individual unity, since it is self-subsisting, nor its internal energy, since it contains within itself all the sources of its energies. The human soul cannot die. Once it exists, it cannot disappear; it will necessarily exist forever, endure without end. Thus, philosophic reason, put to work by a great metaphysician like Thomas Aquinas, is able to

1. Padmanabh S. Jaini, "Karma and the Problem of Rebirth in Jainism", *op. cit.*, p. 219:
   "Even a fully liberated soul (*siddha*), having completely transcended contact with the material realm, is said by the Jainas to retain the shape and size of that body which it occupied at the time *mokṣa* was attained. This latter doctrine is certainly a rather unexpected one, since, even in Jaina terms, total freedom from karmic bonds eliminated the necessity for any limitation upon the extent of the soul. The liberated soul, in other words, could have been seen as *vibhu* without in any way contradicting the Jaina position of the interdependence of the soul and body. One can only conclude that the idea of this interdependence so dominated the minds of Jaina thinkers that they were somehow reluctant to dispense with the body completely even in the case of *mokṣa*. Hence we have a doctrine in which the emancipated soul, though said to be forever free of former influences, seems to display through its shape a sort of shadowy association with the embodied state".
2. M. Hiriyanna, *The Essentials of Indian Thought*, p. 66. Also see p. 65.

prove the immortality of the human soul in a demonstrative manner.[1]

This argument has been criticised both philosophically and psychologically. Kant argued, for instance, that while 'it is true a simple substance cannot disintegrate, consciousness can nevertheless cease to exist through the diminution of its intensity to zero'.[2] It has also been argued, from a psychological point of view "that the words that describe mental characteristics and operations–such as 'intelligent,' 'thoughtful,' 'carefree,' 'happy,' 'calculating' and the like—apply in practice to types of human behavior and to behavioral dispositions. They refer to the empirical individual, the observable human being who is born and grows and acts and feels and dies, and not to the shadowy proceedings of a mysterious 'ghost in the machine.' An individual is thus very much what he or she appears to be—a creature of flesh and blood, who behaves and is capable of behaving in a characteristic range of ways—rather than a non-physical soul incomprehensibly interacting with a physical body".[3]

---

1. As cited in John H. Hick, *op. cit.*, p. 121.
2. John H. Hick, *op. cit.*, p. 121. This argument does not work in Jainism because knowledge is inherent to the soul. Its "knowledge-quality, for example, will increase and decrease, but there is never a time when the soul is without knowledge; otherwise it would became by definition a nonsoul, a material atom" (Padmanabh S. Jaini, *The Jaina Path of Purification*, p. 91).
3. John H. Hick, *op. cit.*, p. 122. The Jaina position on this question if of interest as well. S. Radhakrishnan observes, (*op. cit.*, Vol. I, p. 309-310): "Every jīva is a composite of body and soul, of which the soul is the active partner, while the body is the inactive passive one, Jainism avoids the defects of both mentalism and materialism by recognising the correlativity of mind and matter. But Jainsm does not see that the distinction of self and not-self is the outcome of the essential character of mind. It accepts the two substance theory in all its nakedness, looking upon knowledge as something apart – a process taking place between them. Nor is Jainism aware of the conception of development according to which the body in its higher phases assumes new properties. It is obliged to rest content with a dualism of mind and body and stop at the psychological point of view. It cannot adopt the theory of interaction, but has to accept the view of parallelism with all its difficulties. 'Karmic matter itself through its own essential nature brings about its own changes. Jīva, too, in the same way, through its own impure states of thought that are conditioned by karma, brings about its own thought changes.' The two form two independent series, self-sufficient and complete. To the question, as to why

The Jaina view of the soul obviously needs to be analyzed now, before we can bring a Jain perspective to bear on Plato's views.

Although the soul is immortal according to Jainism, it is so despite the fact that Jainism rejects the two basic grounds for its immortality proposed by Plato: its unchanging nature and its partless nature. These points are philosophically extremely significant, for in adhering to these positions Jainism is 'strikingly at variance with other schools of Indian thought as well, and not just Western thought'.

According to Jainism, the soul is indeed eternal as in Plato, but it "is conceived as an eternal substance (*dravya*) of limited, but variable, magnitude. It is thus capable of adjusting its size to the dimensions of the physical body in which it happens to be housed for the time being. In this latter respect, Jainism is strikingly at variance with the other schools of Indian thought, which conceive of the soul as either atomic or omnipresent and therefore as never changing in size".[1]

Not only is the soul unchanging, according to Plato, it is also not partless. At this point the Jaina doctrine of karma becomes relevant. Unlike the Hindus and the Buddhists, who "take *karma* to be immaterial, the Jains believe it to be but subtle particles of matter, which [finds its] way into the soul...soiling its nature. The implication of this view is that the soul consists of parts for, otherwise, such an ingression of karma particles would be impossible".[2] This view of Hiriyanna may be contrasted with that of

---

the jīva should suffer the fruits of karma, if the two are independent, a sort of pre-established harmony is suggested. In the world we have material bodies large and small, of which some are karmic matter, with a tendency to be attracted by the jīvas. By their coexistence, jīva and karmic material molecules are brought together. The settling of karmic matter in jīva is due to this contiguous coexistence. It cannot be said that the mind exerts an active influence. The commentator on Pañcāstikāyasamayasāra explains the relation by the analogy of the casket which becomes black by contact with collyrium powder. The two self-determining agencies somehow get harmoniously blended. Since direct causal relation between the two series is rejected, no better explanation than a mysterious harmony is possible".

1. M. Hiriyanna, *The Essentials of Indian Philosophy*, p. 61.
2. *Ibid.* Others are content with observing that "Just how a nonmaterial thing can in any way interact with a material one is not well clarified" (Padmanabh S. Jaini, *The Jaina Path of Purification*, p. 114)

S. Radhakrishnan, according to whom "the diffusion of the soul in the body is not like any other diffusion in nature, since the *soul is simple and devoid of parts.* 'Just as the lotus hued ruby, when placed in a cup of milk imparts its lustre to the milk, so the jīva residing in its own body imparts its lustre or intelligence to the whole body'"[1] There is, however, a distinction to be drawn between the diffusion of the soul in the body, and of karma particles in the soul, and there is room for clarification here. At this point the question naturally arises: if the soul is of variable shape and complexion; how, then, can it be said to be eternal? Because, the Jainas suggest, every existent (sat) possesses a quality called *agurulaghutva* ("undergoing neither gain nor loss"). whereby its total number of space-points (*pradeśa*) remains unchanged regardless of the area into which these points must be accommodated. This is described as analogous to a piece of cloth, the total material of which is the same whether it is folded or spread out flat.[2]

Modern interpreters of Jainism also tend to regard the soul as simple (partless).[3]

Jainism does agree with Plato in regarding the soul as immortal, and in its pure state divested of matter. When some Jaina texts say that "the soul exists only within the body",[4] they refer to its empirical state and in that sense the "statement of the text is not quite correct, for the siddhas, the perfect being completely emancipated from karma who dwell in eternal omniscient bliss at the summit of the universe, are souls in a state of complete nakedness, according to orthodox teaching".[5]

Western thought in terms of the body-soul dichotomy, has come full circle now, as it were. According to the Hebrews 'the body was the soul in its outward form',[6] that is to say, the same entity, in terms of its exteriority, was the body and interiority, soul.

1. S. Radhakrishnan, *op. cit.*, Vol. I, p. 311.
2. Padmanabh S. Jaini, "Karma and the Problem of Rebirth in Jainism," *op. cit.*, p. 220.
3. A.L. Basham, "Jain Philosophy and Political Thought" in Wm. Theodore de Bary, ed., *op. cit.*, Vol. I, p. 86. Does it represent modern Platonic influence?
4. *Ibid.*, p. 82.
5. *Ibid.*, note 4.
6. John H. Hick, *op. cit.*, p. 121.

However, in course of time "the body-soul distinction, first formulated as a philosophical doctrine in ancient Greece, was baptized into Christianity, ran through the medieval period, and entered the modern world with the public status of a self-evident truth when it was redefined in the seventeenth century by Descartes. Since World war II, however, the Cartesian mind-matter dualism having been taken for granted for many centuries, has been strongly criticised. As a result of this development, much mid-twentieth-century philosophy has come to see human being as in the biblical writings, not as an eternal soul temporarily attached to a mortal body, but as a form of finite, mortal, psychophysical life".[1]

Neither the Platonic nor the modern view accords fully with the Jaina position, although the Jaina position does, on the whole, lean towards the Platonic view, with some reservations, as indicated earlier. From a Jaina point of view, the modern view collapses matter and spirit too closely – making them the obverse and reverse of the same coin. According to the Jaina view, so far as the soul is concerned, "Knowledge of sentience is its very essence; and empirical knowledge, in its diverse forms, is a manifestation of it under limitations caused by the *ajīva* or inanimate nature – a sort of blinker put upon it during its mundane existence. The eyes, for example, are not viewed as an aid to seeing, but as a check put upon the absolute sight of the soul"[2]—a notion rather at variance with modern ideas of body/mind or body/soul relationship.

The Re–creation of the Psychophysical Person

The question naturally arises: how do these ideas of body-soul interaction relate to one's post mortem existence.

John Hick has developed three scenarios in this context, which help us state this problem in three different settings.

> Suppose, first, that someone-John Smith living in the United States were suddenly and inexplicably to disappear before the eyes of his friends, and that at the same moment an exact

1. *Ibid.*, p. 121, 122.
2. M. Hiriyanna, *The Essentials of Indian Philosophy*, p. 61.

> replica of him were inexplicably to appear in India. The person who appears in India is exactly similar in both physical and mental characteristics to the person who disappeared in America. There is continuity of memory, complete similarity of bodily features including fingerprints, hair and eye coloration, and stomach contents, and also of beliefs, habits, emotions, and mental dispositions.
>
> Suppose, second, that our John Smith, instead of inexplicably disappearing, dies, but that at the moment of his death a "John Smith" replica, again complete with memories and all other characteristics, appears in India. Even with the corpse on our hands, we would, I think, still have to accept this "John Smith" as the John Smith who had died. We would just have to say that he miraculously re-created in another place.
>
> Now suppose, third, that on John Smith's death the "John Smith" replica appears, not in India, but as a resurrection replica in a different world altogether, a resurrection world inhabited only by resurrected persons. This world occupies its own space distinct from that with which we are now familiar. That is to say, an object in the resurrection world is not situated at any distance or in any direction from theobjects in our present world, although each object in either world is spatially related to every other object in the same world.[1]

The first of these is an instance of psychic transportation, the second of reincarnation and the third of resurrection.

The *last* of these is not discussed in Jainism, on account of its highly atheistic orientation.[2] As noticed earlier, Jainism does not

1. John H. Hick, *op. cit.*, p. 123-124.
2. *Ibid.*, p. 124: "What is the basis for this Judaic-Christian belief in the divine re-creation of reconstitution of the human personality after death? There is, of course, an argument from authority, in that life after death is taught throughout the New Testament (although very rarely in the Old Testament). More basically, though, belief in the resurrection arises as a corollary of faith in the sovereign purpose of God, which is not restricted by death and which holds us in being beyond our natural mortality. In a similar vein it is argued that if it be the divine plan to create finite persons to exist in fellowship with God, then it contradicts both that intention and God's love for the human creatures if God allows men and women to pass out of existence when the divine purpose for them still remains largely unfulfilled."

believe in God in the accepted Western sense. The *first* of these is a yogic feat, which is not religiously very significant, however it may be otherwise.[1]

The *second* scenario Jainism treats seriously. Reincarnation results from the fact that the soul is weighed down by karmic particles, otherwise it would naturally ascend to the top of the universe. On account of the ingress of karma, matter permeates the soul and "when karma penetrates the soul it is transformed into eight kinds of prakṛti which make up the karmāṇa śarīra".[2] Four of these, which determine the status of the individual in the next life, are particularly important in terms of the soul's empirical journey: "Āyuṣka or that which determines the length of life in one birth; Nāma or that which produces various circumstances or elements which collectively make up an individual existence, the body with its general and specific qualities; Gotra or that which determines the nationality, caste, family and social standing of an individual; and Antarāya, or that which obstructs the inborn energy of the soul and prevents the doing of good even when there is a desire for it".[3]

Heaven and Hell

Ideas of Heaven and Hell are commonly associated with the post mortem destiny of the person in religions which accept resurrection as well as reincarnation. In Christianity, for instance, philosophically speaking, "It is the promised fulfillment of God's purpose for the individual, in which the full possibilities of human nature will be realized, that constitutes the 'heaven' symbolized in the New Testament as a joyous banquet in which all and sundry rejoice together".[4] Similarly, also religiously speaking, Christianity allows for eternal perdition.[5] However, philosophically, "Just as the

1. Padmanabh S. Jaini, *The Jaina Path of Purification*, p. 153, 256.
2. S. Radhakrishnan, *op. cit.*, Vol. I, p. 320 note 1.
3. *Ibid.*, p. 320 note 1.
4. John H. Hick, *op. cit.*, p. 124.
5. *Ibid.*, p. 124-125. John Hick remarks wryly: "hell, as conceived by its enthusiasts, such as Augustine or Calvin, is a major part of the problem of evil!" (*Ibid.*, p. 125).

reconciling of God's goodness and power with the fact of evil requires that out of the travail of history there shall come in the end an eternal good for humanity, so likewise it would seem to preclude eternal human misery. The only kind of evil that is finally incompatible with God's unlimited power and love would be utterly pointless and wasted suffering, pain which is never redeemed and worked into the fulfilling of God's good purpose".[1]

Jaina thinking on hell seems to follow a similar pattern. Technically, "Jainas have asserted that there exists a class of souls, the *abhavya,* that can never attain *mokṣa*".[2] This would constitute the Jaina equivalent of eternal damnation. It must be noted, however, that this is not in keeping with the general tenor of the liberative eschatology which characterises the Indic religious tradition. In Christianity, salvation is achieved by God's grace and Professor Hick finds the idea of eternal damnation inconsistent with God's goodness and power. It can similarly be argued that salvation or liberation in Jainism is the outcome of one's spiritual endeavour, and any idea of eternal perdition is inconsistent with this belief in the being's infinite power of self-redemption. Surendranath Dasgupta elucidates this point as follows: "It may not be out of place to mention here that though the karmas of man are constantly determining him in various ways yet there is in him infinite capacity or power for right action (*anantavīrya*), so that karma can never subdue this freedom and infinite capacity, though this may be suppressed from time to time by the influence of karma. It is

1. *Ibid.*, p. 125.
2. Padmanabh S. Jaini, "Karma and the Problem of Rebirth in Jainism", *op. cit.*, p. 226. Here it may also "be noted that jīvas according to Jainas are ultimately of two kinds, either bhavya or abhavya. Umāswāmi (VIII-6) seems to hint that *kālāvaraa* [temporal obscuration] is possible in both types of *jīvas* though it may be objected that as abhavya, jīvas have no power of *manaparyāya jñāna* and *kevala jñāna.* This statement is loose. The right view seems to be that a soul is called bhavya or abhavya not because it has or has not a particular *śakti* (*avadhi* or *kevalajñāna*) but because his power can or cannot be manifested by Sāmyagdarśana etc." (Koshelya Walli, *op. cit.*, p. 254 note 2). Also see Padmanabh S. Jaini, "Bhavyatva and Abhavyatva: A Jain Doctrine of Predestination", in *Bhagwān Mahāvīra and His Teachings* (2500 *Nirvāna Anniversary Volume*) (Bombay: 1977) p. 95.

thus that by an exercise of this power man can overcome all karma and become finally liberated. If man had not this anantavīrya in him he might have been eternally under the sway of the accumulated karma which secured his bondage (*bandha*). But since man is the repository of this indomitable power the karmas can only throw obstacles and produce sufferings but can never prevent him from attaining his highest good".[1]

---

1. Surendranath Dasgupta, *op. cit.*, Vol. I, p. 207. Padmanabh S. Jaini's remarks are also helpful here (*The Jaina Path of Purification*, p. 139.) "Jainas grant the soul great powers of manipulation with regard to the karmas. But these powers alone are not considered sufficient to effect the incredible shift from ignorance to insight that makes eventual salvation possible. Such an event, we are told, can occur only in the presence of a further element, an extraordinary quality of the soul called *bhavyatva*, capability to become (free). This quality is said to exist within the soul and yet remain totally untouched by the karmas also present there. It is a sort of inert catalyst, awaiting the time when it will be activated and thus trigger an irrevocable redirection of the soul's energy: away from delusion and bondage, towards insight and freedom.

   The mysterious nature of *bhavyatva* is compounded by the assertion that not all souls possess it. Those which do not are designated *abhavya*; they can never attain salvation. Why the Jainas should harbor such a theory of absolute, permanent bondage for certain beings is not at all clear; it has been dogmatically accepted on the basis of scripture, and may simply reflect the commonplace observation that some individuals show no interest whatsoever in their salvation. Later Buddhist schools (the Yogācāra-Vijñānavādins, for example) held a similar view, comparing such unfortunate beings to 'rotten seeds' forever incapable of spiritual growth". These remarks must, however, also be supplemented with the following to provide the full picture (*Ibid*, p. 141):

   We must bear in mind, however, that for a Jaina the knowledge, bliss, and energy of the soul can *never* be totally extinguished, whereas karmic influence is subject to complete elimination. Hence the soul possesses a sort of *built-in advantage*, an ever present tendency to develop its qualities and temporarily reduce the influence of the karmas. When Jainas say that a soul is free to work for its own salvation, it is this inherent tendency towards self-improvement that is referred to. Thus a soul will again and again progress to transitory states of relative purity and insight, only to be driven back by onrushing karmas, until a moment when the attainment of such a state coincides with the sort of external "activating" conditions mentioned above. We do not know precisely what happens at that moment; it would appear, however, that the bhavyatva is moved to exert its catalytic influence upon the energy quality, thereby redirecting it towards mokṣa. This mysterious event completely alters the future of the soul; its bonds of samsāra begin to unravel, and ultimate salvation is assured.

Jainism and Parapsychology

Parapsychology becomes relevant in the context of human destiny because of "claims that life after death has been proved by cases of communication between the living and the 'dead'".[1] Parapsychology has not been pressed into service for vindicating its doctrines by Jainism in this manner; but, in some other ways, the parapsychological dimension of Jainsm is of considerable interest epistemologically, though perhaps not eschatologically.

It has already been pointed out that the Jainas distinguish between five kinds of knowledge: *mati, śruti, avadhi, manaḥparyāya* and *kevala.* Out of these (1) *mati* "is ordinary cognition obtained by normal means of sense perception"[2] and (2) *śruti* "or testimony is knowledge derived through signs, symbols or words".[3] Of special interest to us here, however, are avadhi, *manḥaparyāya* and *kevala.*

> (3) Avadhi is direct knowledge of things even at a distance of time or space. It is knowledge by clairvoyance. (4) Manaḥparyāya is direct knowledge of the thoughts of others, as in telepathic knowledge of others' minds. (5) Kevala or perfect knowledge comprehends all substances and their modifications. It is omniscience unlimited by space, time or object. To the perfect consciousness the whole reality is obvious. This knowledge, which is independent of the senses, which can only be felt and not described, is possible only for purified souls free from bondage.[4]

This progressive gradation of knowledge and the integral vision of it as consisting of the sensory, the extrasensory and the transsensory possesses a certain elegant clarity. However, the special sources of knowledge, namely, those beyond the sensory are not pressed into service to resolve the issue of life after death,

1. John H. Hick, *op. cit.*, p. 294.
2. S. Radhakrishnan, *op. cit.*, Vol. I, p. 294.
3. *Ibid.*, p. 295.
4. *Ibid.*

which is accepted as a matter of course;[1] what is striking is that *kevala jñāna* or perfect knowledge is accessible in this life and verifies a pre-mortem state, as distinguished from post-mortem existence.

In the samsāra state on account of the karma veils this purity is sullied, and the veils are only worn out imperfectly and thus reveal this and that object at this and that time as ordinary knowledge (*mati*), testimony (*śruta*), supernatural cognition, as in trance or hypnotism (*avadhi*), and direct knowledge of the thoughts of others or thought reading (*manaḥparyāya*). In the state of release however there is omniscience (*kevala-jñāna*) and all things are simultaneously known to the perfect (*kevalin*) as they are. In the samsāra stage the soul always acquires new qualities, and thus suffers a continual change though remaining the same in substance. But in the emancipated stage the changes that a soul suffers are all exactly the same, and thus it is that at this stage the soul appears to be the same in substance as well as in its qualities of infinite knowledge, etc., the change meaning in this state only the repetition of the same qualities.[2]

1. "*Avadhi jñāna* corresponds to what is known as clairvoyance. It is a kind of extra-sensory perception, not ordinarily available to all persons, though it is latent in everyone. Through the instrument of extra-sensory perception, one may actually see events taking place in a distant land or at a distant time. Mnaḥ-paryāya jñāna refers to the knowledge of thoughts in other minds. It has direct access to the mind of other persons, and this capacity arises only as a result of *yoga* or *tapas*". Appaswami Chakravarti, "Jainism: Its Philosophy and Ethics", in Haridas Bhattacharyya, ed., *op. cit.*, Vol. I. p. 427.
2. Surendranath Dasgupta, *op. cit.*, Vol. I, p. 207.

CHAPTER XI

HUMAN DESTINY: INDIC PERSPECTIVES

Introduction

A preliminary observation, which one encounters in many a text-book on comparative religion reads somewhat as follows:

> Together with Buddhism and Jainism, which bear to Hinduism somewhat the same relationship as Christianity and Islam bear to Judaism, Hinduism is sharply distinguished from the religions of the West by its belief in transmigration. The great religions of the world may broadly be divided into two main groups by this criterion, and Hinduism is the oldest and most enduring of the Eastern group, which maintains that the soul inhabits many bodies in its journey through the cosmos, until it reaches its final goal, which is described in varying terms by different sects. The corollary of this doctrine is that all life, whether supernatural, human, animal, insect, or with some sects even plant, is governed by the same law. Whereas Western religions generally teach that man is a special creation, *possessing an immortal soul which is denied to the lower animals*, Hinduism maintains that all living things have souls, which are essentially equal, and are only differentiated through *karma*, or the effect of previous deeds, which conditions the integuments of subtle and gross matter imprisoning the souls and thus leads to their successive rebirths in different types of body. This doctrine of samsāṛa has given a very distinctive character to much Hindu thought and philosophy.[1]

1. A. L. Basham, "Hinduism", in R.C. Zaehner, ed., *op. cit.*, p. 225.

John Hick puts it more succinctly: '"To nearly everyone formed by our western Atlantic culture it seems self-evident that we came into existence at conception or birth and shall see the last of this world at death: in other words, we are born only once and we die only once. However, to one brought up within a Hindu or Buddhist culture it seems self-evident that we have, on the contrary, lived many times before and must live many times again in this world".[1]

What is said above of Hindu or Buddhist culture also applies to the Jaina.

In his discussion of the idea of karma and incarnation in general, John Hick identifies three distinct, though related, models of this doctrine: (1) the popular concept; (2) the Vedantic concept and (3) the demythologized interpretation. This trichotomy is also helpful in presenting the Jaina discussion of the theme and so we will let the present discussion also flow along these customary channels.

Popular Conception

The popular conception of reincarnation on the Indian subcontinent can be related to the numerous stories of people, especially children, who claim to remember a previous life. Such stories keep surfacing in India. One such well-known case is of "Shanti Devi: Lugdi–who was born in 1902, lived in Mathura, and died in 1924 as Mrs. Chaubey–was (presumably) very different as regards both physical and psychological descriptions from Shanti Devi, who was born in 1926 and lived in Delhi. But Shanti Devi claimed to have certain memories of people and events experienced by Lugdi, which are said to have been confirmed by impartial investigators. Our reincarnation hypothesis is that despite the differences between them, they are in fact the same person or self,...In speaking in this way of the same person being born in 1902 in one part of India, later dying, and then being born again in 1926 in another part of India, we are presupposing the existence of a continuing mental entity which I am calling the self or the person".[2]

With the help of this case, John Hick raises the crucial question:

1. John H. Hick, *op. cit.*, p. 130.
2. John H. Hick, *op. cit.*, p. 133.

how is the identity of this entity through time – across lives – to be established? He starts his examination of this issue by raising a simpler question first: how is the identity of a person even during the course of a single life established? He illustrates the issue autobiographically as follows:

> Consider the relation between John Hick who is now writing, whom I shall call J.H.66 and the John Hick at the age of two, whom I shall call J.H.2. The main differences between them are, first, that J.H.66 and J.H.2 do not look at all like each other and, second, that their conscious selves are quite different. As to the first difference, no one shown a photo of J.H.2 would know, without being told, that it is a photo of J.H.66 as he was sixty-four years ago; for there is very little similarity of appearance between these two visible objects. As to the second difference, if one were to hear a recording of the two-year-old J.H. revealing his thoughts in words and other noises one would, I think, feel that J.H.66 has a very different mind. No doubt the same basic personality traits are present in both the child and the man, but nevertheless the conscious self of the one is very different from the conscious self of the the other-so much so that a comparison of the two would never by itself lead us to conclude that they are the same self. There are, then, immense differences between J.H.2 and J.H.66 from the points of view both of physical and of psychological description. *Notwithstanding that, J.H.66 does have at least one fragmentary memory of an event that was experienced by J.H.2. He remembers being told when his sister, who is two years younger than himself, was born. Thus there is a tenuous memory link connecting J.H.66 with J.H.2 despite all the dissimilarities* that we have noted between them; and this fact reminds us that it is possible to speak of memory across the gap of almost any degree of physical and psychological difference.[1]

His basic argument is that while such a memory-link resolves the conceptual difficulties involved in defining identity in the

1. *Ibid.*, p. 132-133, emphasis added.

course of a single life, "the idea of reincarnation in the sense of the transmigration of the self *without memory* of its previous lives from death in one body to birth in another is beset by conceptual difficulties".[1]

The importance of the memory-link becomes clear, once an attempt is made to establish identity over several lives on grounds other than those of memory. How, in the absence of memory, could such a claim be postulated? John Hick argues that identity across a life may be woven out of three strands: (1) physical continuity; (2) psychological or dispositional continuity and (3) memory. If memory is removed from the scene and the physical bodily link is snapped by death, then dispositional continuity survives as the sole remaining criterion. But this is too vague to serve as a criterion, for on this basis "I could equally well be a reincarnation of any of many thousands of people in each past generation. Thus, this criterion of character similarity is too broad and permissive; if is establishes anything, it establishes much too much and becomes self-defeating".[2]

---

1. *Ibid.*, p. 135, emphasis added.
2. *Ibid.*, p. 135. The preceding observations may also be cited with benefit here (*Ibid.*, p. 134-135. "Thus, all that is left to be the bearer of personal identity is the third strand, which is the psychological continuity of a pattern of mental dispositions. It is this that now has to carry all the weight of the identity of two persons, one of whom is said to be a reincarnation of the other. For the only connection left, when memory and bodily continuity are excluded, lies in the psychological dispositions that constitute one's personal character. It is claimed that B, who is A reincarnated, has the same personality traits as A. If A was proud and intolerant, B will be proud and intolerant. If A becomes in the course of her life a great artist, B will start life with a strong artistic propensity. If A was kind and thoughtful, B will be kind and thoughtful. But much now depends, for the viability of the theory, upon the *degree* of similarity that is claimed to exist between the total personalities of A at t^1 and B at t^2. Many people are kind and thoughtful, or have artistic temperaments, or are proud and intolerant, but as long as they are distinct bodily beings with different and distinct streams of consciousness and memory, the fact that two individuals exhibit a common character trait, or even a number of such traits, does not lead us to identify them as the same person. In the case of people living at the same time, to do so would be a direct violation of the concept of 'same person'. In the case of people who are not alive at the same time such an identification is not ruled out with the same a *priori* logical definitiveness; but it is nevertheless beset with the most formidable difficulties. For the similarity between A (t^1) and B (t^2) must, in most cases, be so

The Vedantic Conception

The Vedantic conception goes beyond the empirical being as consisting of merely body and mind and postulates a soul. Upon this assumption "Each psychophysical ego is...a temporary expression, or organ, or instrument of an eternal soul, one indeed of the succession of such expressions which constitute the successive rebirths of that soul. That the soul is involved in māyā means that it has become enclosed in a set of 'bodies' or coverings, thought of on the analogy of a number of sheaths successively enclosing the blade of a sword, and all having to be discarded before the blade is free".[1] The "sets of bodies" just alluded to need to be identified now. "There are three such principal 'bodies' or sheaths: the gross body (sthūla śarīra), the subtle body (sūksma śarīra or liṅga śarīra), and the causal body (kāraṇa śarīra). So far as the essential logic of the idea of rebirth is concerned, we can combine

general as to be capable of numerous different exemplifications, since A and B may be of different races and sexes, and products of different civilizations, climates, and historical epochs. There can be *general* similarities of character, found in such qualities as selfishness and unselfishness, introverted or extroverted types of personality, artistic or practical bents, and in level of intelligence, between, let us say, a male Tibetan peasant of the twelfth century B.C.E. and a female American college graduate of the twentieth century C.E.. However, such general similarities would never by themselves lead or entitle us to identify the two as the same person. Indeed, to make an identity claim on these grounds – in a case in which there is neither bodily continuity nor any line of memory – would commit us to the principle that all individuals who are not alive at the same time and who exhibit rather similar personality patterns are to be regarded as the same person. But in that case there would be far too many people who qualify under this criterion as being the same person. How many people of Lugdi's generation were as much like Shanti Devi in general character as Lugdi was? Probably many hundreds of thousands. How many people in the last generation before I was born had character traits similar to those that I have? Probably many hundreds of thousands. On this basis alone, then it would never have occurred to anyone that Lugdi and Shanti Devi were the same person, or that I am the same person as any one particular individual who lived in the past. On this basis I could equally well be a reincarnation of any one of many thousands of people in each past generation. Thus, this criterion of character similarity is far too broad and permissive; if it establishes anything, it establishes much too much and becomes self-defeating."

1. *Ibid.*, p. 136.

the latter two into one, the 'subtle body', and concentrate upon the relation between this and the 'gross body'. The 'gross body' is the physical organism that begins to be formed at conception and begins to disintegrate at death. It is survived by the 'subtle body', which then influences the development of another physical body as its next vehicle of incarnation".[1] Be it noted that the use of the word "body" here is potentially misleading to a Western ear, for this body is really immaterial in nature.[2] The process of rebirth may now be summarized as follows:

> So far as its function in the theory of rebirth is concerned, we may describe the liṅga śarīra as a mental entity or substance that is modified by, or registers and thus metaphorically "embodies," the moral, aesthetic, intellectual, and spiritual dispositions that have been built up in the course of living a human life, or rather in living a succession of human, and perhaps also nonhuman, lives. These modifications of

1. *Ibid.*
2. As John Hick explains (*Ibid.*, p. 136-137): "It must, however, at once be added that the phrase 'subtle body' is likely to be seriously misleading to the western mind, for the 'subtle body' is not, in the philosophically sophisticated versions of the theory, conceived of as a material entity in the western sense of 'material.' It does not occupy space, has no shape or size, and is indeed not a body at all in our western sense of the term. It is, however, material in the quite different sense given by the fundamental Indian dichotomy between consciousness and everything that lacks consciousness and is called *prakṛti*-'nature' or 'matter'-this being identical with māyā. In western terms the subtle body must accordingly be described as a mental rather than as a physical entity; indeed, one Hindu expositor speaks of it simply as 'the psychical part of the psychophysical organism.'" The point is further clarified later (*Ibid.*, p. 137) as follows: "We have already noted that the subtle body belongs to the material (*prakṛti*) side of the fundamental dichotomy between consciousness and *prakṛti*; and it is for this reason that it is appropriate in the context of Indian thought to call it a body. For being finite, changeable, and devoid of consciousness, it has far more in common with the physical body than with the soul. To appreciate this we have to conceive of thoughts, emotions, and desires as things, and as things capable of existing apart from consciousness, as dispositional energies that, when linked with consciousness, can guide action. Through like grouping with like in mutual reinforcement, such dispositions form relatively stable and enduring structures whose 'shape' is the character of the person whose thoughts have formed it."

> the subtle body are called saṁskāras, impressions. But they are not thought of on the analogy of static impressions, like marks on paper, but rather as dynamic impressions, modifications of a living organism expressed in its pattern of behavior[1]+Such a dispositional structure survives the extinction of consciousness in death and continues to exist as an entity, the subtle body or liṇga śarīra, which will later become linked to a new conscious organism.[2]

This account of reincarnation must be distinguished from why this account is to be considered credible. "If we ask *why Hindus believe that this is a true account* of the facts of human existence, there are three interlocking answers. One is that it is a revealed truth taught in the Vedas. A second is that reincarnation is a hypothesis that makes sense of many aspects of human life, including the inequalities of human birth... The third is that there are the fragmentary memories of former lives to which we have already referred, and also, even more important, the much fuller memories that are attained by those who have achieved mokṣa, liberation and enlightenment"[3]

Although Hindu and Jaina thought shares a general belief in the doctrine of karma[4] and reincarnation, there are several specifics with regard to which they differ, and it is time to bring these differences into sharper focus.

---

1. *Ibid.*, p. 137. John Hick clarifies the nature of saṁskāras further as follows: "We would ordinarily think of the human mind and personality as being modified in all sorts of ways by its own volitions and its responses to its experience. A repeated indulgence in selfish policies reinforces one's egoistic tendencies; a constant exercise of the discipline of precise thought makes for more lucid and exact thinking; devoted attention to one or another of the arts quickens and deepens one's aesthetic sensibilities; spiritual meditation opens the self to the influence of a larger environment; and so on. These familiar facts can be expressed by saying that the *liṇga śarīra* is the seat of the various emotional, spiritual, moral, aesthetic, and intellectual modifications that are happening to us all the time in the course of our human existence. Such modifications are most adequately characterized in contemporary western categories as mental dispositions".
2. *Ibid.*
3. *Ibid.*, p. 138.
4. Vasudha Narayanan, *op. cit.*, p. 153.

(1) One must begin with the concept of the soul itself. By this word the Jainas "understand *only* the individual self, and not the supreme soul of the Upanishads"[1] *Brahman.* Thus Jainism, though acknowledging that "even material entities have their own souls", "does not believe in any universal spirit or God in the common acceptation of the term".[2]

(2) The difference extends not only to the existence of *Brahman* but also to the nature of the Ātman or the individual soul, in terms of its size, qua soul. As Padmanabh S. Jaini points out: "A significant issue in Indian philosophy concerns the actual *size* of the soul. Virtually all the Vedic *darśanas* assert that the soul is *vibhu,* omnipresent; Rāmānuja's theory of an *atomic, dimensionless soul is the only orthodox exception to this view.* An all-pervasive soul would of course be free from spatial limitation by the body; indeed, the very idea of 'dimensions' cannot be applied to such an entity at all. Jainas, however, have consistently rejected the *vibhu* theory, arguing that since a soul cannot experience the sorrow or happiness resulting from its karma except in the context of mind, sense, and body, any existence of the soul outside that context becomes incompatible with the function of the karmic mechanism. This line of thought leads directly to the basic Jaina doctrine that a soul is exactly coterminous with the body of its current state of bondage (svadehaparimāṇa)".[3]

(3) The differences between Hinduism and Jainism are not restricted to the spiritual plane, in the context of the doctrine or karma and reincarnation. The differences incarnate themselves on the material plane as well: "Jain and Hindu views of *karma* differ in one important way: the Jains consider *karma* to be material in nature. It is said to exist as undifferentiated subtle matter particles. These particles become attracted to the soul when the being thinks, speaks, or acts in any way. Karmic matter seems to be specially attracted to souls that are 'moist' with desires; the drier, more dispassionate souls are not so easily polluted. Particles of karmic

1. M. Hiriyanna, *The Essentials of Indian Philosophy,* p. 60.
2. *Ibid.* For its reason for rejecting *Brahman,* see Wm. Theodore de Bary, ed., *op. cit.,* Vol. I, pp. 81-83; for rejecting God, *Ibid.,* pp. 78-81; etc.
3. Padmanabh S. Jaini, "Karma and the Problem of Rebirth in Jainism", *op. cit.,* p. 219.

matter stick to the soul and keep it in a state of bondage. Over births, the souls become coloured with the type of *karma* they are polluted by; the darker the soul, the more soiled it is with negative *karma*. This is a far cry from the purity and crystalline nature of the liberated soul".[1]

(4) Jainism has a concept analogous to that of the liṅga śarīra in Hinduism. Although in some ways their form and function are similar, in other ways they are different. The liṅga śarīra, as the karma-bearing unit, has a functional and formal parallel in the Jaina concept of kārmaṇaśarīra and is often explicitly mentioned as such;[2] "at the same time it differs in form inasmuch as it possesses both weight and colour[3] (unlike the liṅga-śarīra as usually described) and its function is not merely to convey the soul from one body to another but prevent it from simply flying upwards, as an unencumbered soul would in Jainism, to the summit of the universe".[4] The point may be further clarified as follows:

> For the system to work, in other words, the karmic "channel" must exist in some manifest, if subtle, form in which the soul is contained. This is in fact exactly what the Jainas have claimed; the transmigrating soul is said to be housed by a "karmic body" (*kārmanaśarīra*), as well as by a so-called luminous body (*taijasa-śarīra*). The former is composed of the sum total of one's karma at a given moment; the latter acts as a substratum for this karmic matter during the *vigraha-gati* and also functions to maintain body temperature during gross physical existence. Both of the invisible bodies are said to suffuse the gross and visible one during life; thus they not only "convey" the soul from one birth state to the next but constitute a real physical link between these states as well.[5]

(5) In Hinduism, questions regarding the time the soul spends between two incarnations and the nature of its intervening existence[6] are handled in various ways.

1. Vasudha Narayanan, *op. cit.*, p. 153.
2. Hiralal Jain, "Jainism: Its History, Principles and Precepts", *op. cit.*, p. 407.
3. *Ibid.*
4. Padmanabh S. Jaini, "Karma and the Problem of Rebirth in Jainism", p. 230.
5. *Ibid.*, p. 230-231.
6. P.V. Kane, History of Dharmaśāstra (Poona: Bhandarkar Oriental Research Institute, 1977) Vol. V., Part II (second edition) p. 1551-1561.

The Jaina position on this, however, is distinct and uniform: such transmigration is instantaneous. This is confirmed by two very different approaches: one philosophical, the other sociological. Padmanabh S. Jaini points out: "Committed as they were to the doctrine that the *vigraha-gati* typically occupies only a single moment, Jaina thinkers faced one major difficulty, namely, explaining how the 'choice' of exactly appropriate circumstances for the next rebirth could possibly be made in so short a time. (Recall, in this connection, the *gandharva's* lengthy 'search' for a proper birth-environment.) They have dealt with this problem by positing the existence of a unique factor, the so-called āyuḥ ('longevity') *karma*".[1] He also notes that whereas Jainas "have adopted many Hindu customs and ceremonies pertaining to such things as marriage, the coming of the new year, childbirth, and so forth, they have *never* taken up what is perhaps the most important of all rituals in Hindu society, namely, *śrāddha,* the offering of food by a son to the spirit of his dead parent".[2] The reason is obvious: "It will be apparent that for Jainas the very idea of *śrāddha* is doctrinally invalid; a soul which goes to its next body in one moment cannot be fed, propitiated, or dealt with in any other way by those left behind".[3]

(6) .The Jainas attach more doctrinal significance of the idea that the last moment of the previous existence determines the next. The idea is not absent in Hinduism but has been contested.[4] However, since the next incarnation is virtually instantaneous in Jainism, the soul has to be on "get, set" at the end of the previous life itself, all set to "go". Thus "Although emphasis on the religious significance of the last moments of life is by no means unique to the Jainas (similar notions prevail among Hindus, Buddhists, and certain non-Indian communities as well), it might be said that the idea of *āyuḥ-karma,* on the basis of which Jainas rationalize this emphasis, is unique. But this idea itself is not a fundamental one;

1. Padmanabh S. Jaini, "Karma and the Problem of Rebirth in Jainism", *op. cit.*, p. 233-234
2. *Ibid.*
3. *Ibid.* Also see p. 229 note 27 and P.V. Kane, *op. cit.*, p. 335-339
4. P.V. Kane, *op. cit.*, Vol. V, Part II, pp. 972-973, 1598

it seems to function, as we have seen mainly as an explanatory adjunct to *the* distinctive Jaina doctrine pertaining to rebirth, namely, the momentariness of *vigraha-gati*".[1] Hence *āyuḥ-karma* comes to acquire special significance in the Jaina scheme of karma and reincarnation. It "functions in a most unusual manner. *Every other sort of karma* in the Jaina system is said to be in a constant bondage (*bandha*) and fruition (*anubhāga*) relationship with the soul; some *nāma-karma*, for example, is at every moment being bound, to come to fruition at some future time, while another is at every moment producing its result and falling away (*nirjarā*) from the soul. *Āyuḥ-karma*, however, is bound *only once* in a given lifetime, and its fruition will apply only to the very next life".[2]

(7) This produces another domino effect. Jainism identifies one's karmic legacy as consisting of eight elements: four bearing on the soul and four on the body. The former are called "'vitiating' (*ghātiyā*) karmas, which effectively keep a soul in bondage",[3] such as ignorance[4]; the latter are called *aghātiyā* (not so) and include the following: "(i) *nāma-karma*, a cover term for the collection of karmic material whose fruition determines some ninety-eight different aspects of the future body, for example, its destiny or class of existence (human, animal, etc.), its sex, color, number of senses, conformation of limbs, and the like; (ii) *gotra-karma*, controlling whether the environment into which one falls is or is not conducive to the leading of a spiritual life; (iii) *vedanīya-karma*, producing either pleasant or unpleasant feelings in response to the environment, hence the level of happiness or unhappiness which characterizes an individual; (iv) *āyuḥ-karma* whereby the exact duration of life (ostensibly measured, among human beings, by the number of breaths to be taken) is established".[5]

The point of this enumeration is to indicate how, on account of its special role, *āyuḥ-karma* trumps the rest: "This specificity of application effectively places *āyuḥ-karma* in a position of primacy relative to the other *aghātiyā* karmas, since these must 'fall into

1. Padmanabh S. Jaini, "Karma and the Problem of Rebirth in Jainism", *op. cit.*, p. 233
2. *Ibid*, p. 232.
3. *Ibid.*, p. 231.
4. *Ibid.*, note 32.
5. *Ibid.*, p. 231-232.

place' in conformity with the life-period that has been fixed. Given an āyus of seventy years, for example, only those *nāma-karmas* generating rebirth in a destiny where such a life-span is appropriate could conceivably come into play. Thus it is that the 'selection' of the particular aghātiyā karmas determinative of the next existence occurs *before the moment of death.* There need be no 'search' during the *vigrahagati,* since all 'choices' have already been made".[1]

(8) Some schools of Hindu thought, such as that of Vedānta, identify God as in charge of the "moral administration of the universe"[2], as it were, and thus supervising the working of karma and reincarnation. Jainism makes no such assumption. "The Jaina thinker is a staunch believer in karma as his friend the Buddhist is, but he does not recognize his necessity of positing a supreme conscious person for the administration of karma. Hence though Ācāryas like Kunda-kunda, and others believe in Paramātmā they do not believe in Īśvara either as a creator or as a universal teacher (Guru)".[3] It is a curious fact that in this respect the so-called "unorthodox" school of Jainism provides a point of convergence with the most orthodox school of Hindu philosophy, the Mīmāmsā.

(9) In Hinduism and Buddhism, the liberated ultimately lose all trace of individuality in our conventional sense, but the Jaina state of perfection or *siddhi* "should not be considered analogous to the concept of nirvāna of the Buddhists or the Brahman of the Vedantins. For according to the Jainas, even in this condition, traces of individuality persist".[4]

(10) The actions performed by the perfected beings, while alive, are karmically non-binding as much in Jainism as in Hinduism and Buddhism. "Sāmantabhadra in his Brhatsvāyambhūstotra says—'O' Lord! The activities of thy Body, Mind and Speech are not by Will, nor even without deliberation. Thy activities are unthinkable. This shows that the activities of the body, mind and speech of Lord

1. *Ibid.*, p. 232.
2. Koshelya Walli, *op. cit.*, p. 308.
3. *Ibid.*, p. 307.
4. Koshelya Walli, *op. cit.*, p.264. She goes on to say: "The bodies of the Siddhas are supersensuous, free from fatigue, mutually impenetrable and blissful. The Siddhas have no bodies of their own which are due to karma. Their bodies are auspicious and glorious. In the Uttarādhyayana sūtra (Chapter XXXVI, 52-58), it is stated that the Siddhas are separated from Alokākāśa and are

(Bhagavān) have no will or Īcchā behind them and no judgment. His activities are unthinkable".[1]

In Hinduism, this karmically free action is associated with liberated beings and sometimes also with God, or his Incarnations. In Jainism, on account of its non-theistic nature, it is associated with liberated beings, in whose case "due to right knowledge even bhoga whether enjoyment or suffering does not become a source of bondage. This shedding of karma is both material and psychical. It is said that a man of true knowledge is not adversely effected by the action of pudgala karma, is not bound down or directly influenced by karma. It may be remembered that this view of the Jainas is exactly the view of the ancient post-Vedic ideas. It is illustrated in the so called ocean-churning described in the Mahābhārata in which the deadly poison was swallowed by Śankara and yet instead of falling prey to death, he conquered it and became Mrtyuñjaya. Even the devas were unable to swallow the deadly poison which Śankara with His Infinite power assimilated into Himself".[2]

One question still remains to be answered: on what grounds do the Jainas subscribe to the doctrine of karma and reincarnation? In the case of Hinduism the answer was transempirical, empirical and psychological. It was revealed truth; it offered rational explanation of inherent inequalities and the memory of past lives could be recovered through yoga.[3]

---

established from the top of the lokākāśa. They leave behind them their laukika bodies here and become Siddhas there. It is further stated that the Siddhas rise up beyond the *vimāna* namely *savārtha* and are settled in a place which looks like an umbrella. This place is known by the name of Īṣatprāgbhāra. Very interesting descriptions of this are found in ancient Āgamas.

Beyond this place is the farthest end of the mundane world. Even the Siddha deha is not the same as the ultimate body of the soul. The Ācāryas say that it represents two third of the ultimate body. Speaking from the viewpoint of an individual, Siddha state is with a beginning but without an end. Speaking from the collective view point, it has neither beginning nor an end".

1. *Ibid.*, p. 255.
2. *Ibid.*, p. 257
3. It may be worth noting that (1) "The Jains consider memory (*smti*) as a pramāṇa and class it under non-perceptual knowledge, but the Buddhists do not contribute to this idea" (Narendra Nath Bhattacharyya, *infra*, p. 175)

The Jaina response focuses on revelation more that the rest. This might sound odd, as the warrant for faith in revelation would presumably come from God and Jainism is atheistic.[1] In the Hindu case the warrant lay with the self-revealing character of the Vedas. The Jainas, however, believe neither in this view[2] of the Vedas nor in the Vedas themselves.[3]

Jainas accept belief in karma and reincarnation because these doctrines are found in their scriptures and Jainas believe in their scriptures because they represent the teachings of omniscient beings.[4]

A Demythologized Interpretation

A third approach John Hick adopts towards the doctrines of karma and reincarnation is to treat the doctrine as "a mythological expression of the fact that all our actions have effects on some part of the human community and have to be borne, for good or ill, by others in the future".[5] For arriving at this interpretation he relies on J.G. Jennings' interpretation of Buddha's interpretation of the Hindu teachings on karma and rebirth.[6] J.G. Jennings writes:

> Disbelieving in the permanence of the individual soul he [the Buddha] could not accept the Hindu doctrine of Karma implying the transmigration of the soul at death to a new

(2) According to Jainism, "The soul is directly perceived by introspection just as the external things are" (Surendranath Dasgupta, *op.. cit.*, p. 188) and (3) Karma for the Jainas "has a special significance. It is the key to the understanding of all the unexplained facts of life and universe"(Narendra Nath Bhattacharyya, *op. cit.*, 147).

1. *Ibid.*, p. 203-206.
2. *Ibid.*, p. 188.
3. *Ibid.*, p. 186.
4. *Ibid.*, p. 186. On the nature of this omniscience, see Padmanabh S. Jaini, *The Jaina Path of Purification*, p. 266-267. Does the distinction between Jaina and Buddhist doctrines of omniscience imply that while a Buddha may become aware of any past life, *one at a time*, a Jaina Arhat may be aware of all *simultaneously*?
5. John H. Hick, *op. cit.*, p. 140.
6. J.G. Jennings, *The Vedāntic Buddhism of the Buddha* (London: Oxford University Press, 1948).

> body; but believing fully in moral responsibility and the consequences of all acts, words, and thoughts, he fully accepted the doctrine of Karma in another sense, implying the transmission of the effects of actions from one generation of men to all succeeding generations.[1]
>
> x x x
>
> Assuming the common origin and the fundamental unity of all life and spirit, he [the Buddha] assumed the unity of the force of Karma upon the living material of the whole world, and the doctrine of Karma taught by him is collective and not individual.[2]

There is no doubt that this constitutes a morally imaginative understanding of the doctrine of karma and reincarnation. However, from a Jaina point of view, it runs into two difficulties. The first of these is that such an understanding assumes a doctrine in which karma works itself out 'corporately' rather than individually. The Jaina understanding of the working of karma, however, is highly individualistic, even more so than in its Hindu and Buddhist versions. The second difficulty in accepting a demythologized interpretation of the Vedantic doctrine of karma and reincarnation lies in the fact that it is possible to offer a demythologized interpretation of the Jaina doctrine of karma and reincarnation itself!

The Jaina emphasis on a highly individualistic understanding of this karma has already been alluded to. This individualism explains why the Jainas did not adopt the Hindu custom of śrāddha, in which the son makes offerings to nourish the departed-because it implied that one individual's karma (the son's) could somehow influence someone else's (i.e. the father's) state of well-being. According to the Jaina view, only one's own actions could influence one's destiny.[3] The following lines of a tenth century Jaina teacher, Amitagati, may also be cited in support of this position. They almost celebrate the fact of karmic indivisibility.

1. Cited by John H. Hick, *op. cit.*, p. 140.
2. *Ibid.*
3. Padmanabh S. Jaini, "Karma and the Problem of Rebirth in Jainism", *op. cit.*, p. 233-234

Whatever karma a soul has acquired through its own prior deeds
it will obtain the good and bad results thereof.
If one could obtain results from the deeds of others,
then surely his own deeds would be meaningless.

Except for karma earned for oneself by oneself
no one gives anything to anyone.
Reflecting upon this fact, therefore,
let every person, unwaveringly,
abandon the perverse notion that
another being can provide him with anything at all.[1]

Thus, if one takes the Jaina doctrine of karma and reincarnation on its own, then the demythologized Vedantic interpretation of karma remains highly problematical. At this point, however, the impediment acts as a stimulus. It seems within the realm of intellectual possibility to entertain a demythologized version of the Jaina doctrine of karma and reincarnation itself.

A move in this direction is made possible by a dimension of the Jaina doctrine of karma and reincarnation, which was only alluded to briefly earlier. It has to do with the classification of beings at various "levels of existence".[2] Jainas affirm birth-categories of four kinds: "gods, men, hell-beings and tiryañcas ('those going horizontally', e.g. animals)". Among the animals they start by distinguishing between animals which possess five senses (e.g. mammals) or lack them (e.g. insects). One then moves down the scale to beings who possess four, three, two and finally one sense only, the tactile.

1. *Ibid.*, p. 235. Padmanabh S. Jaini goes on the say (*Ibid.*, p. 235-236): "This emphasis on reaping the fruits only of one's own karma was not restricted to the Jainas; both Hindu and Buddhist writers have produced doctrinal materials stressing the same point. Each of the latter traditions, however, developed practices in basic contradiction to such a belief. In addition to śrāddha, we find among the Hindus widespread adherence to the notion of divine intervention in one's fate, while Buddhists eventually came to propound such theories as the boon-granting *bodhisattvas*, transfer of merit, and the like. Only the Jainas have been absolutely unwilling to allow such ideas to penetrate their community, despite the fact that there must have been a tremendous amount of social pressure on them to do so".
2. *Ibid.*, p. 223.

These single-sensed beings are of five types, possessing bodies of (1) earth, (2) water, (3) fire (4) air or (5)vegetable life.

This last category subdivides into those examples in which one soul is associated with only body, and those in which the souls are "at so low a level that they do not even possess an individual body, but rather exist as a part of cluster or 'ball' (golaka) of organisms of the same type".[1]

The spot of light you see at the end of this classificatory tunnel is the light leading into another classificatory tunnel. These entities, referred to above, called *nigoda*, are of two kinds: (a) *nitya-nigoda* and (2) *itara-nigoda. Itara-nigoda* are those which result from souls ending up in this state on account of their rotten karma, while *nitya-nigoda* consists of existents which have not yet risen to the dignity of a soul. The word *nitya* usually means 'eternal' but here "always up to now" would be appropriate.[2]

Now the question arises: "what can it mean to say that there are certain souls which have *always* been *nigodas*?" The answer runs as follows. Souls in the realm above are finite though "incalculable so the question arises: will not this universe lose all sentience with the departure of the souls, speculatively speaking? The answer is: this will not happen because souls from the *nitya-nigoda* will rise to the occasion.

Padmanabh S. Jaini has offered the following demythologized explanation of this phenomenon.

> Given the Jaina admission that *some* souls begin their existence in this rather primordial and undifferentiated state, we may not be wrong in inferring that such could be the case for *all* souls. Adding to this the fact that every soul is said to exist along a virtual continuum of consciousness, from the minimal but ineradicable trace of awareness (*nitya-udghātita-jñana*) possessed by the nigoda to the omniscience i.e., kevalajñāna) of the *siddha*, we have here a model which is both linear and evolutionary in its conception.[3]

1. *Ibid.*, p. 224.
2. *Ibid.*, p. 225.
3. *Ibid.*, p. 227. "It should be noted, however, that this is not a theory of necessary evolution; the Jaina also accepts the possibility of retrogression, and thus of eternal bondage" (Padmanabh S. Jaini, The Jaina Path of Purification, p.111).

RECOMMENDED READING

Surendranath Dasgupta, *A History of Indian Philosophy*, Cambridge: Cambridge University Press, 1951, Vol. I.

Padmanabh S. Jaini, *The Jaina Path of Purification*. Berkeley, California: University of California Press, 1979.

Bimal Krishna Matilal, *The Central Philosophy of Jainism* (Anekānta-vāda), Ahmedabad: L.D. Institute of Indology, 1981.

S. Radhakrishnan, *Indian Philosophy*, New York: The Macmillan Company, 1929, Vol. I.

Walther Schubring, *The Doctrines of the Jainas*. (Tr. Wolfgang Beurien), Delhi: Motilal Banarsidass, 1962.

Nathmal Tatia, *Studies in Jaina Philosophy*, Varanasi: Jaina Cultural Research Society, 1951.